T0322725

Thomas J. Lipton's
America's Cup Campaigns

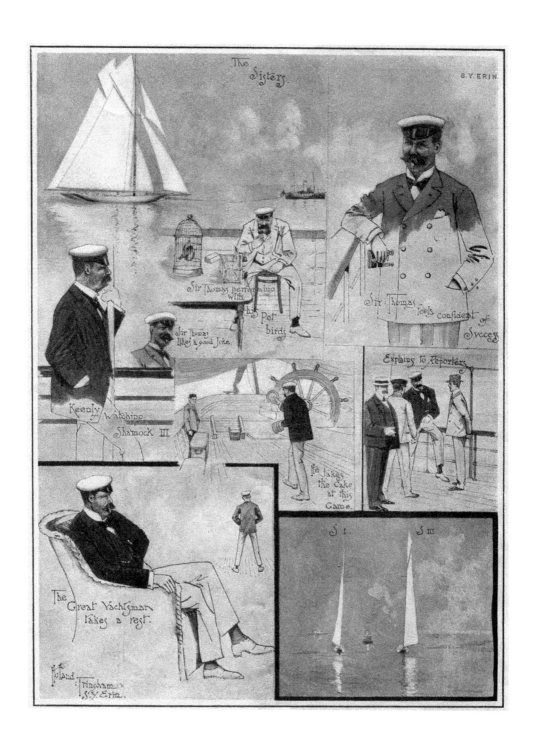

The Sisters

S.Y. ERIN.

Sir Thomas performing with his Pet birds.

Sir Thomas likes a good Joke.

Sir Thomas feels confident of Success

Keenly watching Shamrock III

Explains to Reporters

He takes the Cake at this Game.

The Great Yachtsman takes a rest.

Roland Tringham S.Y. Erin.

S I.   S III

THOMAS J. LIPTON'S
AMERICA'S
~CUP~
CAMPAIGNS

THE SAGA OF ONE MAN'S THREE-DECADE
OBSESSION WITH WINNING THE
AMERICA'S CUP

RICHARD V. SIMPSON

FONTHILL

Frontispiece: Sketches of Sir Thomas J. Lipton. (*Graphic courtesy of Steve and Michelle Mascena*)

Fonthill Media Language Policy

Fonthill Media publishes in the international English language market. One language edition is published worldwide. As there are minor differences in spelling and presentation, especially with regard to American English and British English, a policy is necessary to define which form of English to use. The Fonthill Policy is to use the form of English native to the author. Richard V. Simpson was born and educated in the State of Rhode Island, USA and now lives at Bristol RI, therefore American English has been adopted in this publication.

Fonthill Media LLC
www.fonthillmedia.com
office@fonthillmedia.com

First published 2015

ISBN 978-1-62545-101-9

Typeset in Minion Pro 11pt on 16pt
Printed and bound by CPI Group (UK) Ltd, Croydon, CR0 4YY

Contents

PREFACE   7

INTRODUCTION   8

1   Challengers and Defenders since 1870   13

2   Passing of the 70-foot Class   17

3   Designing a Cup Yacht   25

4   Safety in a Cup Yacht   29

5   Development of the 90-foot Racing Yacht   32

6   Thomas J. Lipton, Tea Merchant   41

7   The Herreshoff Defenders (1893–1937)   45

8   The Shamrock Challengers   81

9   1899, *Shamrock* vs. *Columbia*   95

10   Why the *Shamrock II* Cannot Win   108

11   1901, *Shamrock II* vs. *Columbia*   113

12   1903, *Shamrock III* vs. *Reliance*   127

13   1920, *Shamrock IV* vs. *Resolute*   139

14   1930, *Shamrock V* vs. *Enterprise*   147

15   The Finishing Touch   160

APPENDIX   165

ABOUT THE AUTHOR   169

BIBLIOGRAPHY   171

ENDNOTES   172

Author's Note

I T IS ALWAYS INTERESTING and informative to read the comments and predictions of contemporary sport writers a century or so after first appearing in print. For this narrative about Lipton's *Shamrock* challengers and Herreshoff's defenders, I have resurrected many long-forgotten contemporary sport writers' accounts relative to late nineteenth- and early twentieth-century yachts built especially as America's Cup racers.

Throughout this book, details on yacht dimensions and race statistics are drawn from various sources of the period including newspaper reports, scientific journals, books, and sport magazines. The identities of authors of long sequences of directly quoted text are acknowledged when known; typically, this quoted text is in the public domain.

Preface

T HE EYES OF THE world's yachting fraternities linger lustily in admiration over the celebrated trophy considered the blue ribbon prize of the yachting world.

In fact, the America's Cup is as useless as an old tomato can because it has no bottom, so it does not hold liquid.

When the *Thistle* came over in 1887 (to be beaten by the *Volunteer*), the Scotch syndicate which built that eminent cutter imported a Highland piper, of great celebrity to sound on his instrument enthusiastic praise and rapturous joy celebrating the capture of the coveted Cup. The piper with confidence of success said he would drink Scotch whisky out of the Cup before it left America. The dejected piper would not believe the Cup was bottomless until a steward of the New York Yacht Club showed it him. It is written he muttered a few choice words in Gaelic, presumably an imprecation. Indeed, from the patriotic Scot's point of view, a hollow mockery.

Introduction

S IGNIFICANT EVENTS HAPPEN DAILY, although at the time of their
happening their significance is not recognized. Therefore, let us
consider the advent of yacht racing in America at the early date of
1845. Describing the racers as yachts may be a bit over-generous. Most of
the craft in these days were not the luxury craft we envision today. These
early boats were workboats: pilot boats, packets, fishing schooners and
general harbor workboats with less than luxurious crew quarters.

It was from the anchorage in the Hudson River opposite the New York
Yacht Club's first clubhouse that the start of the first regatta took place on
July 17, 1845. Generally, being an unknown sport to the public at large,
prerace publicity of the event drew thousands of spectators to the banks
of the river to view the novelty of sailboat racing.

The entrance fee of five dollars, paid by the nine boats starting, bought
the prize of a silver Cup, which no doubt the owner of the schooner *Cygnet*,
which carried off the honor, was very proud of his victory.

Imagine a fleet of smart-looking sail boats of varied beam and draft
at anchor off the shore, with cables hove short, and all canvas except the
head sails extended to a rattling southerly breeze. All hands alert for the
starting gun—some at the windlass, others at the jib and foresail halyards;
the captains with their eyes riveted on the muzzle of the club cannon as
the time for the start draws closer.

Suddenly, a flash of flame, a puff of smoke, a loud, reechoing report and
the captains bellow "Up with the anchor, boys; heave with a will. Hoist
away the headsails!" In a moment, like a flock of great white water birds,
the entire squadron is under way, and with a fine heel to port or starboard,
the boats are beating seaward. Many a conflict is fought between eager

friendly rivals anxious to be the first to round the spit and first to set his spinnaker for the run home.

Then the joy of victory and raucous good-natured fighting of the battle continuing in the clubhouse accompanied with smoking and knocking-down glasses of grog, which is the custom of all hearty seafaring men.

While the sport of sailboat racing was new to America, it had a long established tradition in Britain. For decades, the Royal Yacht Squadron (RYS) partook in friendly member racing challenges.

When in 1851, the Royal Yacht Squadron's annual regatta around the Isle of Wight coincided with Prince Albert's First International World's Fair, the RYS offered the trophy, purchased and presented by the Marquess of Anglesey, Sir Henry Paget, as the prize to the winner of the regatta.

Upon receiving the invitation to join the competition, J. C. Stevens and G. L. Schuyler of the New York Yacht Club contracted construction of the keel schooner yacht *America*.

Fifteen vessels: eight cutters, and seven schooners sailed the race, held at Cowes, on August 22, 1851; the race and the Cup was won by the yacht *America*. Because of the victory, the Cup has ever since been referred to as the America's Cup.[1]

After Commodore John C. Stevens, his brother Edwin and Colonel James A. Hamilton, son of Alexander Hamilton, brought home the Royal Yacht Squadron's Cup, the tall silver ewer graced the drawing room in the Commodore's home on Washington Square. There gathered the little coterie of men who had financed the voyage of the *America* to discuss plans for the Cup's disposition, one of which being of melting it down into six medals for the owners of the yacht.

The Cup's first notable public appearance was at a banquet at the Astor House on October 1, 1851, tendered by the New York Yacht Club honoring the adventurous yachtsmen whom Columbia College President King toasted as "Our modern Argonauts, they have brought home, not the Golden Fleece, but that which gold cannot buy—national renown."

The genial Commodore after relating the story of the Cup's capture handed it around among the members of the syndicate in attendance. At dinner's end, the Cup reverted to the club, dumped into a carpetbag, and Secretary Nathaniel Bloodgood carried it to his home in Greenwich Village. Because he neither placed any great monetary value on the trophy nor had any particular regard for its significance is shown by after some time it became hidden behind a stack of books and papers, and lay for years tarnished and all but rejected.

Tradition tells us it was Secretary Bloodgood's sister Maria who rescued the Cup from obscurity; tradition also says it was she who suggested placing it before the sporting world as an incentive to international yachting. The survivors of the syndicate accepted the suggestion, George L. Schuyler being the principal in bringing the plan forward.

During the following 48 years, many tried but all failed to wrench the Cup from the halls of the New York Yacht Club. In 1870, the British yacht *Cambria* lost to the *Magic*; 1871, the *Sappho* defeated the British challenger *Livonia* ; 1876, the *Madeleine* defeated the *Countess of Dufferin*; 1881, the Canadian yacht *Atalanta* lost to *Mischief*; 1885, the cutter *Puritan* won over England's *Genesta*; 1886, the *Mayflower* beat England's *Galatea*; 1887, and the *Volunteer* whipped Scotland's *Thistle*.

The races in 1893 and 1895 are noted for the scandalous behavior of the haughty Irish Lord Windham Thomas Wyndham-Quin, the Earl of Dunraven. In 1893, Nat Herreshoff's *Vigilant* thrashed the Earl's *Valkyrie II*. The 1895 contest between Herreshoff's *Defender*[2] and Dunraven's *Valkyrie III* ended when the Earl quit the race claiming a disruptive spectator fleet and cheating on the part of the defending yacht. Dunraven's bad behavior and unsportsmanlike attitude left a bad taste with the world's

The Herreshoff Manufacturing Company designed and built the 1895 champion sloop the *Defender* for the Iselin and Morgan Syndicate.

The George Watson designed 1895 106-ton, 125-foot cutter challenger, the *Valkyrie III.*

yachting fraternity. Unfortunately, for Dunraven, his legacy in yachting history is as a quitter and spoiled sport.

It is true that crowding of the racecourse in New York Bay was a hazard for competitors and spectators alike. Because of this the races were relocated into the Atlantic off Sandy Hook, New Jersey, but even on the rolling seas, the course was lined with large excursion steamers and ferry boats packed to the rails with an audience of thousands of paying passengers.

However, in 1899, a new contender issued a challenge and a series of five races over thirty-years established a new chapter of sportsmanship; those are the *Shamrock* challenges of Sir Thomas J. Lipton. Lipton's 1899 challenge revived good feelings toward British yachtsmen.

Though defeated, Lipton returned four more times over the following three-decades with bigger and faster boats. All five Lipton challenges came through the Royal Ulster Yacht Club of Belfast, and all five were named *Shamrock*, with the usual Roman numeral after the first. Turning first to one designer and then to another, Lipton ordered boats without fear. He did not interfere in their design when they were in commission or in their management by sailing on any of them in a Cup race.

The first *Shamrock*, designed by William Fife, Jr., was easily defeated in the first and third matches, by the Herreshoff-built, bronze sloop *Columbia*. The *Shamrock* withdrew from the second after losing her topmast.

Two years later George L. Watson produced the *Shamrock II*, and the *Columbia* again called upon, was able to repeat her champion victory although her margin in the last race was only by 41 seconds. The third *Shamrock* was soundly defeated in 1903 by the galloping *Reliance*, the largest of the Cup defending Sloops. The next *Shamrock* designed by Charles Nicholson, was on her way to the scene of the races when the European war broke, and the contestants did not engage until 1920.

Three yachts were built to meet the 1920 challenge: the *Resolute* designed by Herreshoff for a New York syndicate; the *Defiance*, created by George Owen for Boston, New York, and Philadelphia yachtsmen; the *Vanitie*, designed by William Gardner for Alexander S. Cochran.

The *Defiance* withdrew after the 1914 trials, and the *Resolute* was selected defender after a lively series with the *Vanitie* off Newport.

Lipton came within striking distance of a Cup win in his fourth effort in 1920, the *Shamrock IV* winning the first match because of an accident to the *Resolute*, and taking the second on a fluke. It was only the deft hand and cool brain of the then current U.S. Navy Secretary, Charles Francis Adams, who saved the Cup. After two bad starts, Adams tied the score, and worked the *Resolute* into the lead in the fifth race winning by the largest margin in a Cup race in forty years.

1899   Sir Thomas Lipton's *Shamrock* loses to Herreshoff's *Columbia*, 3-0.

1901   Herreshoff's *Columbia* wins again 3-0 over *Shamrock II*.

1903   Sixteen thousand square feet of sail on Herreshoff's *Reliance* triumphs over Lipton's *Shamrock III*.

1920   Lipton challenges with *Shamrock IV* winning two but lose three straight against Herreshoff's last Cup Defender, the *Resolute*.

1930   With masts as tall as 165 feet and hulls over 80 feet in length the boats of the J-class debut. Vanderbilt's *Enterprise* meets Lipton's new entry the *Shamrock V* in Rhode Island Sound winning 4-0.

CHAPTER ONE

Challengers and Defenses since 1870

T ODAY, MANY SAILBOAT-RACING ENTHUSIASTS skip lightly over the
gap of 34 years from the first of the memorable series of matches
to the *Puritan–Genesta* race in 1885, as if that was the first race
in which the Cup was contested. The 1885 race is often referred to as the
beginning of the modern era; however, the first Cup race between sin-
glestickers was that between the *Atalanta* and the *Mischief* in November
1881. The quandary is because the *Atalanta* was a Canadian yacht, and
the contest between British-built cutters and American sloops really
began with the 1885 race.

Two English schooners and one from Canada had tried their prowess
before the advent of the *Atalanta*. The first was the *Cambria*, which came
over in the summer of 1870 and battled with the New York Yacht Club's
fleet as the *America* had battled with the Royal Yacht Squadron, during
the fateful race around the Isle Wight, but not with the sane success; the
Cambria finished eighth by actual time and tenth by corrected time.

The *Livonia*, owned by James Asbury, of the Royal Harwich Yacht Club,
came over next, and on October 18, 1871, sailed the first of a series of
five races. The *Columbia*, owned by Franklin Osgood, was selected Cup
Defender. The course was from Stepleton, around Sandy Hook Lightship
and return. The *Columbia* won by 25 minutes 18 seconds. The *Columbia*
also won the next race by 11 minutes 33 seconds; in the third race, she
lost her flying jib, and the *Livonia* won by 15 minutes 10 seconds. Because
of this loss, the *Sappho*, owned by W. P. Douglass, was substituted for
the *Columbia*. She proved to be too much for the English boat, winning
the fourth race by 30 minutes 21 seconds and the fifth by 25 minutes
27 seconds.

Then the Canadian yacht the *Countess of Dufferin*, owned by Charles Gifford of the Royal Canadian Yacht Club came seeking the Cup. The defender was John S. Dickinson's *Madeleine*. This was a scheduled three-race affair, but the *Madeleine* made short work of the matches run on August 11 and 12, 1876, winning the first by 10 minutes 14 seconds and the second, which proved to be a rout by the *Madeleine* winning by 27 minutes 14 seconds.

In 1881, the *Atalanta* came down from the Royal Canadian Quinte Yacht Club seeking to capture the Cup by challenging Joseph R. Busk's *Mischief*. There was one match race sailed over the inside course and there was another 16 knots to windward and return. Sadly, the Canadian was not in racing trim and lost the first race by 28 minutes 30 seconds and the next by 21 minutes 6 seconds.

In 1885, trial races were run to determine the best boat to defend the Cup. The *Puritan* defeated the *Priscilla*, both built especially for the defense; she also beat the older boats the *Gracie* and the *Bedouin*. The fifth attempt to take the Cup was by Sir Richard Sutton, with his cutter *Genesta*, he met the *Puritan* and was defeated in two races, though in the second race by only a small margin.

The next challenge came quickly, in 1886, from Royal Navy Lieutenant William Henn with his cutter called the *Galatea*. Unhappily, for Henn, the *Mayflower* in two races more easily beat his boat than was the *Genesta* by the *Puritan*. In the trial races of that year, the *Mayflower* beat the *Puritan*, the *Priscilla,* and the newly built *Atlantic*.

The seventh attempt to recapture the coveted Cup was in 1887, by James Bell with the Scottish syndicate's cutter the *Thistle*. The Boston-based, Edward Burgess-designed *Volunteer* soundly scuttled the *Thistle* in two races.

The next challenge sailed in 1893 by Lord Dunraven with his cutter the *Valkyrie II*. His boat was defeated in three straight races by the Herreshoff designed and built *Vigilant*, which had defeated the *Colonia, Jubilee* and *Pilgrim* in the series of trial races to select a defender.[3]

In the first race of this series, the *Vigilant* came in five and three-quarter minutes ahead of her competitor amid wild applause from a tremendous fleet of spectators. The second race was sailed on October 9, under blustery wind conditions of thirty-miles per hour much of the time, and the *Vigilant* won by 16 minutes 35 seconds. The third contest sailed on Friday the thirteenth was one in which the *Valkyrie* split two spinnakers and suffered various other incidents of bad luck. The American boat also had her share of bad luck with the jib topsail halyard fouling, only an innovative fix saved the day with the defender managing to creep in ahead of the challenger by two minutes 13 seconds, after allowances were made winning by 40 seconds adjusted time.

In 1894, Dunraven built another *Valkyrie*, which unfortunately sank in a storm. Determined to return the Cup to Britain, Dunraven returned to America with *Valkyrie III* in 1895.

Like Ashbury twenty years earlier, Lord Dunraven came back to an equally embarrassing defeat in 1895 with another Watson production, the *Valkyrie III*. For the 1895 challenge, the New York Yacht Club turned again to Herreshoff, who designed and built a composite boat, the *Defender*, which proved equal to the task of sinking the hopes of the British Lord; *Defender* swept the three races by decisive winning times.

The unfortunate result of the Lord's embarrassing defeat were charges of unfairness and cheating against his opponent. A long investigation ensued, the outcome of which was Dunraven's subsequent expulsion from the New York Yacht Club and his indignant departure from the American shore.

A review of the *Defender–Valkyrie III* races by a contemporary writer summed up the races as "a fluke, a foul, and a fizzle." A commentary agreed to by many who witnessed the humiliating defeat and bad behavior of the challenger.

Five seconds after the foul of the *Defender* (right) by the *Valkyrie III* in the September 10, 1895 race.

The New Your Yacht Club's Newport Station, circa 1889.

CHAPTER TWO

The Passing of the 70-foot Class

THE EVENTS OF THE yachting season of 1901 and 1902, and the performance of the 90-foot *Independence* and her sister yachts the *Neola* and the *Weetamoe* more than proved their sailing ability, thus enjoying a greater number of days of sailing than did the one season of competitive sailing by the Herreshoff 70-footers.

By the end of the decade, the 70-footers, the *Virginia* became a houseboat, the *Rainbow* converted into a schooner, and the *Mineola* laid idle year after year gathering barnacles; these once beautiful craft were no longer loved or sailed.

The seventies were tall craft, graceful and fleet. The mighty Atlantic welcomed these handsome sloops as they spread their flawless canvas to the summer winds. Now they are a memory, they have passed, taking their place in the annals of American yachting history.

Lawrence Perry expresses his sentiments about the seventies in his March 1909 Yachting Magazine essay.

Graceful they were, yes; and beautiful and swift; but withal they had their shortcomings, as we view them in the light of these latter day of "wholesome boats," so called. Designed and built as racing machines, they served the purpose for which they were constructed; but at a cost not only to themselves but also to the sport in general. Viewing the sport from the standpoint of ethical purity, I do not consider this an unfair statement.

For the present, I think the average yachtsman will agree that you cannot work up much respect for a boat, which in a bobble of a sea opens its seams, fills with water, and does other unseaworthy things. And neither can you develop much enthusiasm over a class whose first year of racing

The *Yankee* Launched May 10, 1930 by the Yankee Syndicate: John Lawrence, Charles Francis Adams, and Chandler Hovey. The *Yankee* nearly beat the *Rainbow* in trials for the honor of defending the Cup in 1934.

A 1934 view of the J-class yacht *Rainbow* at the Herreshoff yard in Bristol, RI where she is being prepared for the forthcoming America's Cup elimination trials. Photograph by Acme News Pictures, Inc.

was characterized, partially at least, by an all-absorbing desire to win, with consequent evasions of rules, bickering, charges and counter-charges, until much of the good that might have resulted from this important class was swallowed up in regrets.

No class of large racing yachts ever made its bow to the salt sea under more favorable conditions, under auspices more promising. The *Columbia* had successfully defended the America's Cup the preceding year, and the stimulus, which this event had imparted, to the sport in this country was at its height. The old Cup-racer *Vigilant* was in commission and racing; so was the English yawl *Ailsa*. The first of the invading 60-foot English cutters was spreading canvas to the winds of the Sound. Racing spirit was keen, and the pick of our yachtsmen had not yet given ear to the siren call—which is to say, the honk-honk of the racing motor car.

The time, the opportunity for great deeds was ripe. Enter the seventies! Out of Bristol, they sailed, as graceful as beautiful women picking their way along a ballroom floor. There were four of them—*Mineola*, built for August Belmont; *Rainbow*, built for Cornelius Vanderbilt; *Virginia*, built for W. K. Vanderbilt, Jr., and *Yankee*, built for Harry Payne Whitney and Herman Duryea. They were built by the Herreshoffs on a one-design basis, and suggested a merging of the lesson learned from both *Defender* and *Columbia*. They had much greater area of fin keel in proportion to waterline length than *Columbia*; their fins, in fact, were nearly as long as *Columbia's* although of some five feet less in depth. Their underbodies were deeper than *Columbia's* and the midship sections were strongly suggestive of *Defender*. Overall, they were interesting boats, suggestive of advancement in the science of the racing machine.

By the last of May 1900, the boats were on the Sound tuning up for the season's racing. Right here the first hiatus occurred. According to William K. Vanderbilt, Jr., it had been the understanding among the four owners that the boats should be sailed in the summer's races by amateurs. Some one surely must have been mistaken, for Mr. Belmont engaged Capt. Wringe, who had assisted in sailing *Shamrock* against *Columbia*, while Cornelius Vanderbilt secured the services of Capt. George Parker, well known as the successful skipper of swift British racing yachts. It is to be assumed that the parties to the understanding were equally divided. At all events, W. K. Vanderbilt sailed *Virginia* throughout the season with a crew of "Scowegians," while Herman Duryea handled the stick of *Yankee*, having before the mast as many native-born Americans as one could wish to see on a reeling deck. The first club race of the class was in the annual regatta of the New York Yacht Club in June. Two of the boats appeared at the line, *Mineola* and *Rainbow*. The start was on New York's lower bay, and before the boats had been underway a great while there came a series of squalls, which were valued, inasmuch as they furnished the first practical test of the theoretical charge that the seventies would not stand up in a breeze of wind. It must be said they acquitted themselves nobly, and dispelled for all time the allegations of tenderness; as a matter of fact, they were never tender, whatever else could be said of them. Wringe and Parker had a battle royal, *Mineola* returning a victor by a little more than a minute.

On June 19, at Glen Cove, *Mineola* repeated her victory, this time by more than ten minutes. Some very sharp and stubborn jockeying marred the start, which might well have landed one or the other of the contestants at the bottom of the Sound. It became perfectly clear that Wringe and Parker were out for mugs and prize money and were going to play the game to the limit. Still, it may well be suggested, what were they there for but just that?

The first important races in which the class appeared intact was the special series of regattas held by the New York Yacht Club off Newport, beginning July 13. Up to that time, *Mineola* had carried everything before her, and the boats, in point of supremacy, were then rated; *Mineola*, *Rainbow*, with the other two craft anywhere or nowhere. The first race was sailed over a 37-mile triangle, starting from Brenton's Reef Lightship. The day was clear, with one of those early easterly winds, so frequently occurring off Newport, which generally turn from south to westerly before the day is over. Herman Duryea, as fine a Corinthian skipper as ever cracked sail, was at the wheel of *Yankee*; W. K. Vanderbilt, Jr., sailed his *Virginia*, while the two professionals were in their accustomed places on the other boats. Duryea, with great acumen, went off toward Narragansett looking for wind and when it suddenly turned southwest-by-south, and fresh at that, he had all he was looking for. He won the race, defeating *Mineola* by more that nine minutes, *Rainbow* by more than ten, and *Virginia*, which finished second, by a trifle over three minutes.

The *Rainbow* is seen here as Cup Defender in the 1934
contest, skippered by Harold Vanderbilt.

It begins to look good for the Corinthians. Here, through a combination
of skill and luck, *Yankee* had won twice in succession against two of the
ablest racing skippers England had produced; and when, a day or so later,
Yankee won the first race of the series of ten regattas for a thousand-dollar
prize offered by the Newport Yacht Racing Association, it seemed that,
despite the imported talent on *Rainbow* and *Mineola*, the two yachts
sailed by the owners would, throughout the remainder of the season do
themselves credit. One of them did, at least, for when the ten races had
been sailed, five in July and five in August, the score stood as follows:
Yankee, 11 points; *Mineola*, 10 points; *Rainbow*, 8 points.

The *sturm and drang* of the July races off Newport were not without
their effect on the hulls of the big racers. Old Ocean has a way of trying
out the handiwork of man with exceeding impartiality, and strange as it
may seem to some, handles a Herreshoff creation with as little respect as
the product of the humblest designer. The reports were that all the four
boats were in a bad way. However, they got the boats patched up on time
for the annual cruise of the New York Yacht Club, in the port-to-port runs
of which *Mineola* took the lion's share of trophies. On September 8 *Yankee*

For the 1930 Cup Defender trials, former U.S. Navy Secretary Charles Francis Adams, at the wheel of Defender candidate the *Yankee*, sails her on the run from Newport to New London. At Adam's right is Morgan Harris.

rounded-to once more, winning the Postley Cup on the sound, and then the famous race of the year—that for the 70-foot class Cup offered by Sir Thomas Lipton—was sailed off Sandy Hook Lighthouse on September 13. It was one of the most lifeless starts ever made. *Yankee* got over first, with *Mineola*, *Rainbow*, and *Virginia* following in the order named, they all hauled to the spinnaker side of their course and a game of "find the leeward mark." It developed that, of the four yachts, *Yankee* was the only boat bearing for the mark from the outset. However, the advantage was not to go to the skillful navigator that day. *Rainbow*, which had blundered far out of her course, caught the first of a freshening puff of wind from the south and romped home a winner by about one hour.

Thus ended the season's racing, the score standings follow:

	STARTS	FIRSTS	SECONDS	THIRDS
Mineola	31	13	7	7
Rainbow	27	8	7	7
Yankee	21	6	5	5
Virginia	21	1	5	7

On October 5 the yachting world was electrified by a letter addressed to the New York Yacht Club by Commodore Vanderbilt, renouncing all the trophies won by *Rainbow* in the past season, on the ground that ballast had been placed in his sloop after she had been measured. He said he was not aware that this was against the rules and assumed all responsibility for the error. The New York Yacht Club, the Atlantic Yacht Club, and the Newport Yacht Racing Association disqualified *Rainbow*, and the prizes won by her would have gone to the other yachts had their owners been willing to accept them, which they were not.

Thus the season of what might be called bickering ended in general gloom, not the least important result of which was that Mr. Duryea and Mr. Whitney withdrew from yachting, selling their boat finally to Harry Maxwell. Neither man could well be spared from the game, nor have their places since been filled. W. K. Vanderbilt, Jr., never took much interest in yacht racing after that season, and while, in "fits and starts," the seventies have been prominent in later seasons, it may be said that they never fulfilled the promise, which the announcement of the formation of the class presaged.

The Cup Defender *Rainbow* is pictured after her thrilling race with the British challenger *Endeavour*, in Rhode Island Sound. A photograph by Acme News Pictures, Inc., dated September 17, 1934.

Sleek British racing machines: the *Britannia*, sister to the *Valkyrie II*;
the *Astra*, a super yacht built in 1928, refitted in 1987 by Camper &
Nicholson; the *Shamrock V*, the first British yacht built to the J-Class
Rule; The *Candida*, a J-Class luxury super yacht built in 1929, refitted
in 1991 by Camper & Nicholson; and the *Velsheda*, This J-Class yacht
was designed by Charles Ernest Nicholson and built in 1933.

CHAPTER THREE

Designing a Cup Yacht

This chapter is an abridged and edited article originally published in *Scientific American*, March 30, 1921.

From the year 1893 until 1920, when six yachts were built for the defense of the America's Cup, the responsibility of designing a defender has rested on one man, the man whose name is identified throughout the yachting world with the fastest boats that have ever hoisted canvas in the International Cup race.

When the task of designing speedy defenders was entrusted to Nat Herreshoff, they were among the safest craft ever to sail. The task of designing and constructing the fragile hull of a 90-footer, and giving it the strength necessary to carry its enormous weight of lead below and its towering spread of canvas above, requires both skill and experience. Experience and an accumulation of proven data are especially valuable for the knowledgeable designer. It is an acknowledged fact that yacht designing, during the Herreshoff 's nearly three decades of Cup defender designs, was not an exact science, not at least in the sense on which bridge construction is concerned. Originally, the yacht-builder was a man of rule-of-thumb methods, and there are even today many points both in the modeling of the boat and in her sail plan, which are determined not by scientific formula, but by the particular fads or prejudice of the individual designer.

One designer prefers bluffer bows and leaner quarters; the other thinks that better results come from a straight sharp entrance and rather full, broad quarters, as in the original *Shamrock*. In one sail plan is seen the cloths running parallel with the leech, in another they crosscut. The controversy as to whether sails should be as flat as a pancake, or whether they should have

All hands on deck, as the
magnificent *Shamrock*
glides through a calm sea on
October 12, 1899.

something of that bagginess in which the English yachtsmen who succumbed
half a century ago to the *America* largely attributed to their defeat is still a
matter of conjecture. One yachting skipper believes in setting up his rigging
perfectly taut. Another believes in the 1899 contest the *Shamrock* lost the
races because the rigging was not slacked up to the degree, which insures
getting the best results out of the sail.

All of which goes to prove that there may be more things in yachting
philosophy than, during these early decades, have yet been dreamed. The
steady increase in speed which has taken place in later years gives reason
to believe that we have by no means reached, in form of hull or in sail
plan, the theoretically prefect racing craft. The more designers of the Cup
defenders, then, the more ideas, the more proved and reliable data, the
more development, and, most important of all, the less possibility that the
successful defense of the Cup will cease with the incapacitation or death of
one individual.

In 1901, two yacht designers engaged in the task of defending the America's Cup. The yacht built from Mr. Crowninshield's designs is of a type that
differs very widely in some respects from what might be called the typical
Herreshoff model. Although no particulars were yet released, it is practically
certain that the new Herreshoff boat will be an improved *Columbia*. It is also

probable, in spite of certain sensational rumors to the contrary, that the new Watson boat which is building at the William Denny & Brothers shipyard will be in all respects a standard Watson craft, the lineal descendant of the *Britannia, Valkyrie, Meteor* and last year's *Sybarita*. There will be far more likeness between the Watson and Herreshoff boats than there will be between the Herreshoff and the Crowninshield craft. As strange as it may seem, it is possible that from a yacht constructer's purely technical point of view, there will be greater interest evinced in a contest between the two American craft than there will be between the Herreshoff boat and the English challenger.

The *Independence* is an attempt to apply to the 90-foot yacht a form of hull, which developed of late years in the keen competition between small craft of 15- and 20-foot waterline. In no branch of yachting has greater ingenuity or freer inventiveness been shown than by the designers of these little "raters." A wide variety of models, many of them positively grotesque, have been built and tested. Boats of great beam and enormous overhang,

J-class 129-foot, steel sloop the *Velsheda* (sail number J-K7) was developed and built by Camper & Nicholson in 1933.

His Majesty's Yacht *Britannia* was built in 1893 for Commodore Albert Edward, Prince of Wales. K1, clearly seen in this photograph, was the Class/Racing number on HMY *Britannia's* main sail. In 1931, she was converted to the J-Class with a Bermuda rig.

flat-ended boats, boats with wing ballast, others with keel ballast, and others with none at all, while out of the competition there has evolved what is known as the scow-form of yacht, which is, for its size, by far the fastest sail-driven craft with a single hull in the world. The "scow" has enormous overhangs, a flat floor and hard bilge, her beam is ridiculously wide; when she is heeled, her model is such that her sailing-length is almost doubled, while the weather half of the boat, lifted often entirely out of the water, is depended upon to give the boat stability. The *Independence* is practically a modified scow form, with the deep fin-keel and lead ballast of the typical 90-footer hung beneath it. When she heels to a breeze, her sailing length will be increased far beyond that of any previous contestant. Unless there is serious difficulty with the steering and control of the boat when there is any weight in the wind, the great spread of sail, which she will be able to carry, coupled with her relatively small displacement, should render her an extremely fast yacht.

CHAPTER FOUR

Safety in a Cup Yacht

This chapter is an abridged and edited article originally published in *Scientific American*, August 19, 1899.

If we except the bicycle, there is probably no product of the mechanic in which the factor of safety is reduced so near to the vanishing point as in that highly developed machine known as the racing yacht. It is estimated that the factor of safety in a light road bicycle when a heavy rider is riding it over rough roads is not over 1⅓. That is to say, when the machine experiences its heaviest jolts the metal is strained to within 25 percent of its ultimate strength. The frequency of broken forks and buckled frames is the price we pay for lightness in a machine, which while strong enough to withstand the ordinary stress of travel, had but little provision for accidents in the way of rocks, curbstones, or collisions. The public is willing to sacrifice a surplus of strength in favor of lightness, and in the case of careful and judicious riders, the sacrifice is abundantly justified.

In competitive yacht construction, the saving of weight is not a matter of choice but of necessity particularly in these latter days of the art, when the principles of design are known so well that in model and sail plan there will be comparatively little to choose between two rival yachts when they meet on the trial course. As far as the designer and builder are concerned, the contest has come to be one of weight-saving in construction; and the engineer can now claim yacht construction as one of the many arts which, like that of practical architecture, have called in his services and availed themselves of his knowledge of strains and the strength of materials.

Sir John Isaac Thorneycroft in England and Nat Herreshoff in America had both achieved reputations in the construction of fast torpedo craft when the inevitable drift of ideas and events in yacht construction drove Thomas Lipton to the one and Oliver Iselin to the other in their endeavor to secure the ideal racing craft.

How closely Herreshoff and Thorneycroft have crept to the danger line in the yachts *Defender*, *Columbia*, and *Shamrock* is suggested by the mishaps, which have overtaken these boats in the course of their respective preliminary trials. In one race, the *Defender* carried away her gaff, in another the enormous strains on the shrouds caused them to eat into the masthead and in a third race the steering gear collapsed. The *Shamrock* at her launch was lightly kissed by the stem of a friendly tug, which left a deep imprint in the frail metal of her hull. Later, out for a trial sail, the breeze had scarcely filled her sails before the halyards parted and the mainsail came down on the funnel. On her first race she carried away her club topsail yard, and immediately after her start for America, something went wrong with her bowsprit and she sailed back for repairs.

Now it is the *Columbia's* turn, this lovely craft, by far the most beautiful that Herreshoff ever turned out, riding on the reliability of that towering stick on which the weight of spars and under the full press of her canvas depends, suffered the embarrassing folding of her steel mast. It was the case of the failing of the weakest link; the link in this case proving to be the port spreader. The spreader is a slight pine stick, which extends some 15 feet laterally at a point near the heel of the topmast and serves to spread the topmast and masthead shrouds and enable them to exert a more lateral and less vertical pull on these spars. When the spreader split, these shrouds slackened, and the enormous lateral pressure upon that towering pile of canvas fell upon the steel mainmast. While the mast was strong enough to stand the compressive strains thrown upon it by the pull of shrouds, forestays, and backstays, it was unequal to the cross bending strain when the shrouds were slacked up, the wooden topmast snapping in two, resulted in the whole mass of sails, rigging, mast, and spars falling over the leeward rail.

There is a lesson in this circumstance that such a shrewd observer as Herreshoff will not fail to learn. While in the larger elements of a yacht, such as the hull and spars, weight may be judiciously saved to within a certain safe limit, there are smaller but very vital elements such as the spreaders, the steering gear and certain details of the rigging, in which extreme economy of material may prove to be the very worst form of extravagance.

John Brown Herreshoff (1841–1915), though totally blind from
the age of 15, managed his own sail and steam boat building
company until his brother, Nathaniel Greene Herreshoff,
(1848–1938), became his partner in 1878.

CHAPTER FIVE

Development of the 90-foot Racing Yacht

I N THE SUMMER OF 1886 when the 90-foot cutter the *Galatea* (her actual LWL was 87 feet, but she is classed with the 90-foot *Independence*) came across the Atlantic to make the second attempt on the part of an English cutter to capture the America's Cup. She and her sister the *Genesta* opened the period of Cup contests, which has been far the most brilliant in the history of the memorable struggle.

Generally, among the many conditions surrounding the Cup contests of yesteryear, there is only one, at least as regarding the dimensions of the yachts, and this is the rule that neither yacht may exceed 90 feet in length on the water line. They may be as deep, as broad, and as long on deck as their designers may care to make them, but in length, while they may be many feet less, they must not be a fraction of an inch over 90 feet. Subject to this restriction, the problem is to design a yacht, which can carry a maximum amount of sail upon a hull that shall have the smallest possible displacement and wetted surface, and shall present the easiest form to drive through the water.

At the time of the *Galatea–Mayflower* races, the American and English yachts varied widely in form. The English cutter being of the narrow beam and considerable depth of body, while the American sloop being of shallow draught and great beam, and depending upon the movable centerboard to give her the proper lateral plane when sailing by the wind. The initial stability of the sloop was large, the center of buoyancy moving out rapidly to leeward as the vessel heeled, and almost automatically maintaining the margin of stability.

In the narrow cutter, the initial stability was small, the center of buoyancy moving but little to leeward as she listed, although the righting moment increased rapidly with every increase in the angle of heel. On equal displacements, the greater initial stability of the sloop enabled her to carry a considerably larger sail plan, and therefore in light air she was invariably faster than the cutter. At higher speeds, however, the finer form of the cutter showed an advantage against the bluffer lines of the sloop; there was less wave-making resistance and, hence, in the second race between the *Genesta* and the *Puritan*, which was sailed in a robust breeze, the cutter was a match for her shallow-bodied competitor.

The narrow beam of the cutter was due to an English rule of measurement that put a heavy tax upon breath, but none upon draught. As soon as this rule was removed and a new rule of measurement based on waterline length and sail area substituted, the English designers reverted to the more generous breath of the original cutter type. For instance, the *Thistle* with a beam of 20 feet 3 inches to a length of 86 feet 6 inches, against the *Galatea's* beam of 15 feet on a length of 87 feet. The *Valkyrie II*, which with her sister the *Britannia*, may justly be termed the type from which the modern racing craft has sprung, showed on a waterline length of 85 feet, a beam of 22 feet 6 inches, and a depth of 17 feet 6 inches. Simultaneously with this lowering of the lead and widening of the beam, the forefoot was cut away, the sternpost and rudder brought well forward of the after end of the waterline, with the result that the wetted surface and, therefore, the frictional resistance of the vessel was considerably reduced.

On the American side, development had been in the direction of deeper draught and a lowering of center of gravity, until in the *Vigilant*,[4] a boat with enormous beam of 26 feet and the deep draught, for a sloop, of 13 feet 6 inches. With such a draught, it was evident that the days of the centerboard were over. In the *Defender*, Herreshoff produced a keelboat of similar contour to the *Valkyrie*, but with 2 feet greater draught. At the time of the *Valkyrie–Vigilant* races the forward and after overhangs of the racing yacht began to reach far beyond the load waterline. In the *Independence* so great had been the development in this direction that the forward overhang reached 27 feet 5½ inches and the after overhang stretched 23 feet 5 inches. These exaggerated overhangs have the advantage of compensating for the increase in beam by permitting the fore and aft lines to be nearly as fair and easy as those of the old cutter type permit.

In comparison of the midship sections that the modern twentieth-century yacht embodies two points of excellence of the cutter and sloop, for it has the low center of gravity of the one and the high center of buoyancy of the other. The bottom of the lead of the *Independence* is 6 feet 6 inches lower than that of *Galatea* and her beam is 8 feet 5 inches greater. Thanks to her great length, her lines are at least as easy, and by carrying the flat floor of the hull well out into the overhang. The *Independence* designer, Mr. Crowninshield, secured the unmistakable advantage that when the yacht heels, even in moderate sailing breezes she lengthens her waterline from 90 to 105 feet. The cutter, on the other hand, lengthens only slightly. The comparison is not made on the same degree of inclination, for the reason that the relative tenderness of the cutter would cause her to heel about 30 degrees of inclination, for the reason that the relative 30 degrees in a breeze which would only incline the cutter-sloop by 20 degrees. With her straight stem the cutter gains nothing when heeled forward and her gain aft, at the given inclination, is not more than a couple of feet.

In considering the form of the *Independence*, in her midship section she possesses all the initial stability of the sloop-type due to her great beam and shallow body, but the height of the center of buoyancy, when the yacht heels is increased by the great lengthening of the waterline and resultant submersion of the full ends of the yacht. Less than 20 degrees of heel, the center of buoyancy of the submerged portion of the hull moves out to leeward until it is 2.75 feet from the vertical axis of the boat and only 2.83 feet below the normal waterline. Compared with the *Columbia* she shows in this respect a remarkable gain; and it is probable, that the center of gravity of the boat is lower than that of the last Cup defender. In this case, the *Independence* will hoist 1,475 square feet of canvas, or 11 percent more sail than *Columbia*, although the *Columbia's* displacement was greater.

The increased power of the cutter-sloop over the cutter is not all attributable to form and distribution of weight. Significant increased power is the result of building materials and construction methods. Considering the hulls of the two boats, although her displacement is less, in bulk the *Independence* is greatly larger than the *Galatea*. She is 30 feet longer on deck, 8½ feet greater in beam, her deck area alone is 2¼ times as great as that of the *Galatea*. Although technically in the same class by virtue of her waterline length, the *Independence* measured by her actual superficial area is a vastly larger vessel.

In the words of the *Scientific American* sport writer, "It must be confessed that the sail plan of the *Independence* is very impressive. We were prepared for an increase over that of the last contestants, but not for such an increase as this."

The cap of the mainmast is 108 feet and the topmast is 150 feet above the deck, and the head of the topsail, when fully employed will be 172 feet 7 inches above the deck. When comparing the *Independence* with the *Shamrock* and the *Columbia* the gain in sail area is in the direction of greater height; in height there is a gain of 11 feet over the *Columbia* and not less than 17½-feet over the *Shamrock*.

The same sport writer reports the English yachting journals are crediting the *Shamrock II* with a base line of 185-feet that is exactly that of the *Independence*, and a mast measurement of 148-feet. At time of launch, it was unknown whether this measurement is over all or it is from the deck. Lipton's craft's boom is given at 112 feet which is 2½ feet longer than that of the *Independence*, but as the measurement from the forward side of the mast to end of bowsprit of the *Shamrock* is said to be 71 feet as against 74.5 feet in the *Independence*.

DEFINING THE PERIODS

We may divide the fifty-five years from 1851 to 1903 into three broadly defined periods of racing yacht types. The first of these extending from 1851 to 1876 might aptly be termed the schooner period. The first of these races held in 1870 is represented on the part of the challengers by the *Cambria*, a deep keel schooner built by the Ratsey[5] boat yard. The *Cambria*, a vessel of 108 feet waterline length, and several of the yachts that sailed against her, beat her by a substantial margin. Mr. Asbury, owner of the *Cambria* sent his schooner the *Livonia* over to challenge for the Cup; she proved to be an improved *Cambria* with a waterline length of 115 feet and a proportionately larger sail spread. She made a better fight for the Cup than her predecessor, winning one race against the *Columbia*.

Strictly speaking, the Canadian challengers, the *Countess of Dufferin* and the *Atalanta*, and the American defenders the *Sappho* and the *Mischief* should be included in the schooner period because as in all previous

Yacht "Cambria."

In 1868, Michael Ratsey built the 188-ton schooner *Cambria* for James Lloyd Ashbury. The *Cambria* was the first unsuccessful challenger attempting to lift the America's Cup from the New York Yacht Club.

contests for the Cup, their designs were by the "rule of thumb" method used by all contemporary designers. It was not until the second period, extending from the *Genesta–Puritan* races in 1885, to the *Valkyrie–Vigilant* contest in 1893 that the modern scientific method of design began. This essential period is marked by the heroic struggles between the English deep keel cutter and the American centerboard sloop; there is no denying that as the deep keel was the honored maxim of the British, the centerboard was the esteemed ideal of his American competitor.

On the British side of the contests, we see in the growth from the *Genesta* to the *Valkyrie II* a development from the narrow beam, large displacement, and moderate sail plan of the typical cutter to the more generous beam, smaller displacement, and greater sail power of the typical late nineteenth-century yacht. While on the American side, there was evidence of a growing appreciation for the value of a deeper body and a heavily balanced keel as against a small amount of ballast stowed within a broad and shallow hull. Thus, comparing *Genesta* and *Puritan*, we see that while the English cutter had a beam of only 15 feet on a draft of 13 feet 6 inches, as compared with a beam for the *Puritan* of 22 feet 7 inches, and a draft of 8 feet 10 inches in *Valkyrie II*. The beam had increased to about the same as the *Puritan*, while the depth of the keel in the sloop

The *Valkyrie III* was the unsuccessful British challenger of the ninth (1895) America's Cup race against the American Cup Defender, the *Defender*.

Vigilant had grown to 13 feet 6 inches—exactly that of the *Genesta* of eighteen years earlier.

The year 1893 was an epoch-making year in the history of the development of Cup yachts. The most significant fact in the *Vigilant* series was the very conclusive beating given to the English cutter by the American centerboard sloop in a memorable race of fifteen miles to windward when the English cutter turned to mark nearly two minutes in the lead.

The end of the centerboard came about after the visit by the *Vigilant* to Britain where she lost eleven out of eighteen races to the *Britannia*, a sister cutter to the *Valkyrie*.

The third phase of yacht construction may reasonably date from 1895 with the building of Herreshoff's *Defender*.

In the *Defender* period, we witness the full recognition of the scientific construction only less important than scientific design. In 1893, Herreshoff introduced the use of bronze in the underbody of the *Vigilant*. However, it was in the *Defender* that the engineer and metal-smith were first given a free hand, while hollow steel spars first made their appearance on both challenger and defender. It is probable that *Defender* was and will always remain the lightest yacht for her size ever to sail. She has also the unenviable distinction of being the only boat built for either challenge or defense that was useless as soon as her racing days were over.

Defender's original mast was of light [weight] wood and weak and had to be replaced. The second mast was much heavier and Mr. Iselin gave us an order for making a steel mast. This was lighter and more satisfactory and was used in the trial and Cup races. This was the first steal mast in racing yachts.

——Nathanael G. Herreshoff

At the beginning, Mr. [Oliver] Iselin tried to persuade *Reliance's* designer to make her an out-and-out scow for the scows were then nearly unbeatable in the smaller classes, but Mr. Herreshoff would not do this for he thought that in the larger classes a scow was slow in light weather. He compromised by making a model that was as long overall as a scow but had nicely modeled, fine ends. I remember very well watching my father cut this model which he did in about two evenings, proceeding very rapidly with the work as if there were no question in his mind as to the exact shape to do the work best. This is in great contrast to the other designers of the period, or since [circa 1963], who generally spent much time in developing several sets of lines and never quite deciding which was best. As *Reliance* was ordered early, and as her shape problem was settled so rapidly, this left plenty of time for the designer to spend an unusual number of hours on the construction and details.

——L. Francis Herreshoff

With the advent of Lipton's *Shamrock* challenges, construction costs increased dramatically due to the use of expensive alloys and high-grade steel.

The first *Shamrock* was a bronze boat with aluminum topsides and deck; in the *Columbia*, she met a boat with bronze underbody, steel topsides, and wood deck. The second *Shamrock* was plated with bronze from keel to rail; the third *Shamrock* returned to steel plating for the hull. The necessary smoothness of her surface was accomplished by use of special enamel paint, each coat being carefully rugged down before the next coat is applied. This resulted in a remarkably smooth surface.

In this last period of Cup yacht designing there was a wonderful development in the size and power of the boats, until the ultimate was achieved in the *Reliance*. As compared with the *Defender* the beam grew from 23¼ feet to 27 feet, and the overhang length from 126 feet to 145 feet, while the sail spread of 12,640 square feet on the *Defender*, thought to be prodigious in 1895, would be insignificant against the towering fabric raised on the *Reliance* with a total of 16,199 square feet. The *Reliance* was built on the belt-frame and longitudinal system, which Herreshoff introduced in the *Constitution*.

THE PASSING OF THE CENTERBOARD

The fate of the centerboard, as far as big yachts are concerned was determined in 1893, when the keelboat the *Valkyrie II* easily whipped the centerboard *Vigilant* in a fifteen-mile thrash to windward against a stiff breeze. The *Valkyrie II* was the first of the 90-footers built on the fin-keel principle, just as the *Vigilant* was the last of the ninety-footers to carry a centerboard.

In 1895, Herreshoff boldly abandoned this time-honored device in favor of the fixed keel; the *Defender* being the first keel "singlesticker" built for the defense of the Cup.

Regarding keels and centerboards, it is satisfactory to know that the *Columbia*, in the few trials, which she had with the *Defender*, has shown, even before she had time to tune up that she appeared to be a somewhat faster boat. The difference, not exceptionally remarkable, may have disappointed some who thought she had not shown a more marked superiority. Perceptive observers in these matters acknowledge it is more difficult to make a gain of five minutes over a thirty-mile course in late nineteenth century era of yacht designing than it was to make a gain of fifteen or twenty minutes in the first dozen years of the twentieth century.

In competitive trials between new and old Cup defenders, remember that the *Defender* is a phenomenally swift boat. In the only satisfactory race between her and the *Valkyrie III*, she won by nearly nine minutes, and the *Valkyrie III* had easily disposed of the *Ailsa,* a Fife-built 90-footer, in a previous contest. This makes the *Defender* fifteen to twenty minutes faster than the *Ailsa*.

The *Scientific American* sport writer speculates, "Now, *Columbia* will probably have about five minutes advantage over *Defender* on a thirty-mile course, and may, therefore, be taken to be from twenty to twenty-five minutes better than the last Fife-built 90-foot yacht. To justify the confident expectations of the owner of the *Shamrock* that she will bring home the Cup, she ought to beat *Britannia* (which was frequently vanquished by *Ailsa*) by at least twenty to twenty-five minutes. Unless she does this in the trial races, we may regard the coming contest with considerable feelings of security."

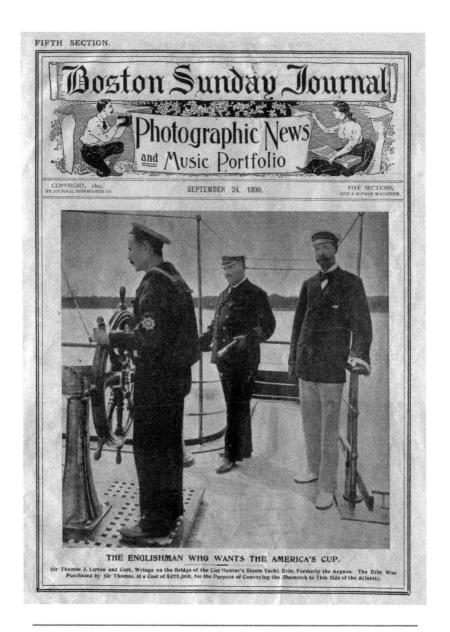

Sir Thomas J. Lipton and Capt. Wringe on the bridge of Lipton's steam yacht the *Erin*. Lipton purchased the vessel fir $375.000 for the purpose of convoying the Shamrock to America for the 1899 Cup races. Photograph courtesy the Boston Sunday Journal, September 24, 1899.

CHAPTER SIX

Thomas J. Lipton, Tea Merchant

THE HUMBLE ORIGIN OF the world's most wealthy tea and grocery merchant is akin to a rise to riches story out of a Dickens' novel. Thomas Lipton (senior), an Irish day laborer and his wife Frances Johnstone were Ulster-Scots. In an effort to better their lives, in 1847 the Lipton family left Ireland and settled in Scotland, young Thomas was born in Glasgow, on May 10, 1848.

By the early 1860s, the Liptons advanced their middle-class lives as proprietors of a small grocer's trade shop where they sold such staples as butter, eggs, bread, and meat.

After about ten years of education at St. Andrew's Parish School, at the tender age of thirteen, Thomas left school to work in his parent's shop and later in a printer's shop as an errand boy. Unsatisfied with low-wage blue-collar labor, he found employment with a tailor as a shirt cutter; during this same period of daytime employment, he continued his education at a night school.

The fourteen-year-old lad, with a youthful thirst for adventure, signed on as a cabin boy on a day-steamer running between Glasgow and Belfast. Shipboard life combined with the stories of seasoned sailors wetted the boy's appetite for further travel experience. Lipton used his saved wages to finance passage on a ship to America.

After landing in New York, he quickly used to his advantage his entrepreneurial wisdom, building capital by his winning personality and willingness to work and learn. The following five years he spent traveling the eastern and southern states working as an accountant and bookkeeper, as a door-to-door sales representative, a farmhand, and perhaps his most inspirational job, which combined all his accumulated knowledge, as a grocery stockman and manager.

Returning to Glasgow in 1870, he rejoined the operation of his parent's small retail grocery store, aiding them with some of the important sales tactics he learned in the States. The following year, after reestablishing himself as a Glasgow resident, he opened his first shop—Lipton's Market— with a full line of provisions. His food market enterprise proved highly successful and little by little, he extended his business establishing a chain of groceries, across Scotland, until he had outlets throughout Britain.

As Lipton expanded his empire of markets, he invested in American stockyards founding a large packing plant; in 1887, he sold the invest-ments—at which we must assume were substantial profits.

During the time he was concentrating on building wealth, the price for tea was falling and a great demand for the beverage was growing among the middle class. Sensing a new market, in 1888 he entered the tea trade and established his tea-tasting bureau, thus bypassing the traditional trading and wholesale distribution network. By cutting out the intermediary, he was able to sell tea at unprecedented low prices thus enabling the poor working class to enjoy the brew.

In order to keep his shops supplied with continuing shipments of fresh tea, Lipton bought tea plantations in Sri Lanka. It was Lipton's import company, which bought the Sri Lanka tea and distributed it through Europe and America.

Therefore, it is that Lipton, through a unique style of shop keeping and imaginative advertising grew a small grocery store into an international business. In 1899, at the age of thirty, the year of his first attempt to win the Cup, he acquired a fortune estimated at $20,000,000.

EVALUATING LIPTON

One of the most interesting figures in international yachting came on the scene in 1899 in the person of Sir Thomas Johnstone Lipton, a wealthy Irish tea merchant; his was the voracious desire to return the Cup to the British Isles.

Turning first to one designer and then to another, Sir Tom ordered boat upon boat without hesitation. Being the solitary financial backer of each boat, he never interfered in their management once they were in commission, and he never sailed on any of them in a Cup race. His persistence, however, won for him the reputation of being a great yachtsman and sporting gentleman, although he readily admitted that he never held the wheel of a yacht in a race.

All five Lipton challenges came by way of the Royal Ulster Yacht Club of Belfast, Ireland, and all five yachts, over a period of thirty-one years, were named *Shamrock*, with the usual Roman numeral after the first.

Although a member of the Royal Ulster Yacht Club, Lipton was not a yachtsman. His five America's Cup challenges awakened lethargic marine sporting men from many maritime nations from their sedentary repose. His first *Shamrock* challenge in 1899, and his continued resolve to sail his *Shamrock* yachts to victory in 1901, 1903, 1920, and 1930, his biographers claim was due to his unquenchable thirst to keep the name Lipton before the eyes of the world. Because of his continuing attempts to win the Cup, Lipton's international tea and grocery business grew beyond the merchant's most wild expectations. A leading British sport journalist called Lipton's challenges, "virtually the finest advertising stunts the world has ever known."

American humorist Will Rogers once wrote of Lipton, "I defy anyone to name a more universally loved character than Sir Thomas Lipton."

Anthony Heckstall-Smith, a friend and social contact of Lipton's said, "He did not go yachting for sport. He went because it was all part of that great advertising campaign to sell Lipton's Tea. No, there can be no doubts that Tommy's repeated attempts to win the America's Cup were virtually the finest advertising stunts the world has ever known. He fooled the entire United States, and most of the world into believing that he was a good sportsman. In the end, I think he even fooled himself."

There is little to believe that when he began contemplating his first campaign to snatch the Cup, that Lipton was not whole-heartedly sincere about winning it. He must have silently mused, "The English lost the Cup, but the Irish will win it." He made his idea of challenging with an all-Irish boat; designed, built, and crewed by Irishmen well known to close friends.

No one took him seriously in 1897, and fewer after his later Cup challenges and defeats. Many English yachtsmen considered him too yacht-ignorant to be regarded seriously. Royal Yacht Squadron members and club officials considered Lipton a *nouveau-riche* mercantile man playing a grand role aspiring to noble rank. Club wags certainly laughed at his complete ignorance of anything of a maritime nature. So ignorant that he could not point out his own boat floating in a pod of look-alike yachts had it not been painted green.

In early 1900, a muckraking rag called *The Glasgow Town Topics* published this mocking portrait of Lipton:

> Since the days of the late lamented Barnum, no such past master in the art of humbugging the gullible public of all nations has arisen and shone with such elegant luminosity. He beats Barnum and goes him one better at least in one respect. The great showman, for the life of him, could not help chuckling and giving himself away whenever his successfully played the populace for suckers. Lipton on the contrary either candidly believes that he is a sportsman and philanthropist or he is the finest actor that ever lived.

Pursued by many women on both sides of the Atlantic, Lipton remained a lifelong bachelor and confirmed homosexual. He was knighted in 1898, became a Baronet in 1902, and he was elected to the Royal Yacht Squadron in 1931. Contemporary yachting-folk familiar with the America's Cup saga continue the laurels of respect granted Lipton for his courteous demeanor and sportsmanship as, one-by-one all five of his *Shamrocks* were defeated.

CHAPTER SEVEN

The Herreshoff Defenders (1893–1937)

A T THE BEGINNING OF his work in 1863, John Brown Herreshoff then only 22 years old, hired a crew of men, procured supplies of seasoned lumber, and fitted out an old tannery as a shop. In the following year, nine sailing craft, ranging in length from 22 to 35 feet, were launched into Bristol Harbor. As his business grew, he bought the old Burnside Rifle Factory, on Burnside Street converting it to a sawmill for producing the enterprise's lumber.

By 1868, Herreshoff Manufacturing had built its first steamer, the *Annie Morse*, followed by the *Seven Brothers*, a pioneer-fishing steamer on the Atlantic Coast built for the Church brothers of Tiverton, Rhode Island.

As knowledge of the Herreshoff brothers' "revolutionary" steam engines spread, they began receiving orders from several foreign governments for "submarine" torpedo boats; the Herreshoffs' were the first torpedo boats built in the United States.

During the late 1870s until about 1883, Nathanael Greene Herreshoff concentrated almost all of his attention on the development of light steam engines and on improving the construction of hulls, trying to reduce weight without sacrificing strength. Practically all of this innovative work was done in connection with the light steam launches the brothers were currently building. Although the alliance of yacht owners originally criticized these early experiments, it is true that many of today's small boats are still built using the construction techniques worked out at the Herreshoff boat yard more than 150 years ago. Proof of the Herreshoffs' authority in this matter is that so many of their small boats, even though lighter in construction than those of his contemporary competitors, are still in use more than a hundred years later.

BUILDING CHAMPION SAILORS

The boat-building firm's partners were John Brown Herreshoff, known as "the blind boat builder of Bristol," and his young scientific-minded brother Nathanael Greene Herreshoff, known as the "Wizard of Bristol", but addressed as Capt. Nat.

Early in the seventies, when the shoal centerboard sloop and the schooner were being developed and perfected, there arose in Bristol, Rhode Island the Herreshoff Manufacturing Company, noted for many speedy yachts, both open catboats and larger-decked craft. By mid-1870s, the Herreshoff yard turned its attention from sailing craft to steam yachts. So engrossed were they in their new enterprise, that they altogether abandoned attention to the controversy regarding the debate surrounding the *Puritan–Genesta* and the Cup races. At the same time, the sailing instincts of Capt. Nat kept him with a keel cruiser anchored off his waterfront home on Bristol Harbor.

Seasoned yachtsmen frequently discussed the abilities of the Herreshoffs as design rivals of Edward Burgess. At the peak of his career, Edward Burgess died; but the genius of yacht designing had not passed with him. Another hand, even more cunning, took up the pencil where he had put it down, and that hand developed novel and winning vessels.

Around the turn of the twentieth-century, many a worried yachtsman came to the Bristol, Rhode Island shipyard of the Herreshoff Manufacturing Co. They came for racing sloops to beat off the British challengers for the America's Cup, and they came to the right place.

John Brown Herreshoff had such an exquisite and singular genius for fine shipbuilding that his blindness was no impediment. He studied all the company's matters in his head and kept countless details of all the vessels he had ever built in his extraordinary brain. Often an assistant would guide him to a vessel on which work was being done, and by putting a hand on the hull, he would give its name.

That twinkle of humor amused J. B. and his visitors, but the record of Cup defenders he and his brother designed and built brought them prestigious customers from 1893 to 1914.

Before the next challenge was received, a new figure in yacht designing had come aboard and a new type of boat had come onto the scene. In the summer of 1891, an odd-looking sloop made her debut in New York waters. Though only 46 feet on the water line she was 70 feet overall. Yachtsmen at first laughed at her long, pig-shaped nose, and flaring convex bows, then marveled at her sailing qualities. Nothing in her class could keep within sight of her. She fairly reveled in rough weather, and could go outside of Sandy Hook and sail a race in a seaway that would stagger a yacht of twice her size; she rode the waves like a duck.

This was the *Gloriana* built for E. D. Morgan, of New York. At this time, the Herreshoff firm had earned a sterling reputation for building fast steam yachts, but had not yet achieved anything of note in building sail yachts.

Capt. Nat's inspiration for the *Gloriana* was a light draft craft used for generations by sports fishermen in Barnegat Bay. He took this as the type for his upper-body and added stability by devising a deep thin under-body, heavily weighted at the foot; the result worked a revolution in yachting.

The following is a reminiscence of the *Gloriana* by Capt. Nat in his own words:

The Gloriana was built and launched early in June 1891. In launching her, ways had to be built, as she was the first deep draft craft constructed by the Herreshoff Manufacturing Company. To save expense, I devise a single ways no wider than the yacht's keel (about 24′) and she slid down safely over it. After the trials were finished, we found we had to put a system of diagonals under her deck to keep it from working. There were no other changes except a pair of truss shrouds, at each forward quarter of the mast, to keep the thrust of the gaff from bending the mast. She was completed and went to New York in time for the June races, and was successful from the start. Mr. E. D. Morgan, her owner, sailed her in the first race, and I sailed her in the seven that followed that season, all of which she won, over the most notable class of that era. At that time, racing measurement was simply length on waterline, with a limit of draft to (16w.1. +1.75). The result was that yachts were being built with enormous overhangs, and elaborate sail plans, as much ballast placed below as possible, i.e. all outside and on the keel. The *Gloriana*'s design had much longer overall length, and more rounding (fuller) waterlines at each end than was usual, giving her a longer body for sailing and the long ends very much decreased the tendency to "hobby horse" and consequently made a much faster and better boat in a sea-way. The general proportion of her rig was probably not as good as her adversaries', but after the June series of races, we had her very well tuned up. She had about 22 tons of lead all outside, and the lightest and best hull, being composite construction, and double planked. While sailing her, I conceived the *Dilemma*, and had her built and tried her out that fall and the following year. From the success of the *Gloriana*, we built the *Wasp* the following winter, for the same class, and for Mr. Archibald Rogers. The *Wasp* was a little faster than the *Gloriana*. Late in 1892, we had an order from Royal P. Carroll for an 85-foot cruising sloop, in which he intended to cruise abroad and do some racing there. Late in that fall, there was a challenge for the America's Cup and quite promptly Archibald Rogers and others gave us an order for the *Colonia*, which was specified to be keel and not over 14′ draft. Mr. E. D. Morgan and others, believing these restrictions unwise, at about the beginning of 1893, gave us an order for the *Vigilant*.

ABOUT CAPT. NAT

In the 1890s, Nathanael, now known as Capt. Nat, favored designing sailing yachts. He hit upon the innovative timesaving idea of building hulls upside-down, with a mold for every frame, and of the lightest possible materials aloft. The firm supplied vessels to the elite of its day, including Jay Gould, William Randolph Hearst, J. P. Morgan, Cornelius Vanderbilt, Harold S. Vanderbilt, William K. Vanderbilt, Harry Payne Whitney and others.

Capt. Nat designed and built a wide range of craft, including the Dough-dish also known as the Bullseye class (originally called the Buzzards Bay Boys Boat), a small sailboat used to train children of yachtsmen. Additionally the *New York 30* class ("30" refers to waterline length), and the 143foot America's Cup behemoth, *Reliance*, with a sail area of more than 16,000 square feet. The 123-foot *Defender* was equally astounding, due to its radical construction; featuring steel-framing, bronze plating up to the waterline and aluminum topsides. As might be expected, when placed in the ocean's saline, the boat's galvanic corrosion was immediate. It won the race, and then began dissolving.

Most designs by the "Wizard of Bristol" have fared better, and today they are highly prized by connoisseurs of classic yachts. The site of the

The *Gloriana* is Capt. Nat's revolutionary redesign of the speedy, sporty sloop. She out sailed everything in her class.. For more on the *Gloriana*, see *America's Cup: Trials & Triumphs*, History Press, 2010.

Herreshoff Manufacturing Company is now a museum dedicated to the preservation of the Herreshoff yachting legacy.

Nathanael Greene Herreshoff is acknowledged as one of the greatest yacht and marine designers and builders that America has ever produced. He brought grace, beauty, and speed to yachting and is credited with the introduction of more new devices in the design of boats than any other marine architect. Literally, he was to yachting what Einstein was to science and what Picasso was to art.

When the *Defender* came out of the Herreshoff yards, this racing sloop of ninety-foot waterline sported many new improvements and novelties in both hull design and rigging, thanks to the inventive genius of Capt. Nat. Four years later, the *Columbia* was launched and was victorious in both the 1899 and 1901 Cup races with Great Britain. The *Reliance* followed in 1903, and then there was the long interval before the *Resolute* sailed to victory in 1920. For the races in 1930, two flyers the *Weetamoe* and the *Enterprise* were constructed at the Herreshoff yard under the supervision of the Company's new owners, the Haffenreffer family. The *Enterprise* was chosen to defend the Cup, and she easily won four of the seven races against Sir Thomas Lipton's *Shamrock V*, sailed in Rhode Island Sound.

During his 72 year career he designed and built five winning America's Cup yachts: the *Vigilant* in 1893 and the *Defender* in 1895, the *Columbia* built for the 1899 competition, which raced again in 1901; the *Reliance* was built in 1903; and the *Resolute* built in 1914 won the Cup in 1920. He sailed them as well, earning a reputation as a most proficient and skilled helmsman. Additionally, the Herreshoff Manufacturing Company built two winning Cup yachts designed by W. Starling Burgess: the *Enterprise* in 1930 and the *Rainbow* in 1934. In short, Herreshoff built every winning America's Cup yacht from 1893 to 1934.

His accomplishments are legend; he designed well over 2,000 craft and produced more than 18,000 drawings. Between 1890 and 1938, yachts he designed won the Astor Cup, Puritan Cup, and Kings Cup; his winning yachts outnumbered the combined wins by all the other yacht designers.

Because of his many accomplishments, he is one of the few people ever made an honorary life member of the New York Yacht Club, his name being listed immediately before His Majesty King George the Fifth and The Prince of Wales.

His fame spread around the world and so greatly did his personality and the yachts he designed dominate the sport, the period of his greatest activity from 1890 to 1920 became known as the "Herreshoff Era." It is undisputed that Nat Herreshoff was a genius and a master, which earned him the nickname the "Wizard of Bristol."

CAPT. NAT'S PERSONA

During conversations with family historian Nathanael Greene Herreshoff III, we discussed several bits of hearsay published by various writers about Capt. Nat's personality. He said:

> I would be very careful in writing about Capt. Nat's personality. Much of what has been written is simply not right. My late cousin Natalie agreed with me about this. I may be the only person still around who knew him well. He lived next door to me until he died when I was seven years old.

NGH III continued with his personal recollections of the strengths and sensitivities of his grandfather. He said, "Capt. Nat was a man of principle."

My grandfather was a very kindly and moral man; he was also very determined and focused; he was of course very organized in whatever he did.

Although the Herreshoffs of Bristol have been devout Episcopalians, as far as I know, Capt. Nat did not have much to do with formal religion. However, I do believe he was a person of definite ideas and beliefs.

Among his closest friends were Frank H. Brown of the Warwick [Rhode Island] branch of relatives, and Commodore Monroe of the Miami area. He was very friendly with the famous yachtsman E. D. Morgan. It was this friendship with Morgan that had much to do with the design of the *Gloriana* and the *Wasp*. Of course, he and the aggressive Scot Captain Charlie Barr[6] had much respect for each other and they worked well together.

The family subscribed to the *Herald Tribune* for weekdays and the *New York Times* on Sunday—because the *Times* had better yachting coverage. The *Times* has always been my best research source when writing yachting history.

One particular story relates Nat's commitment to his belief in his yacht designs. A customer of distinction ordered a new design from the yard after his boat was soundly defeated in a regatta. Nat sent a sketch for a boat with a deeper keel. To which the customer replied it was unacceptable because the water in the harbor was too shallow to accommodate it. Nat replied, "Recommend dredging." The customer was German Kaiser Wilhelm II.

Capt. Nat was a quiet man, not prone to jocular or angry outbursts. It appeared he liked his own company better than the association of many friends. Because his head was evidently full of new plans, he did not have to depend on anybody but himself for entertainment. Judging by the number of new ideas, he evolved and published to the world. In the course of his years of work in Bristol, he must have been "thinking up" something new during most of his waking moments. He walked along the town's streets with his head inclined forward, as if he were in search of some novel notion. There was a local tale that he acquired the habit from watching his rivals in his races, craning his head in order to see them from under the boom.

Capt. Nat's large comfortable home at Bristol, called Love Rocks is built as sturdily as one of his yachts. The house, though altered over the years, still stands facing west into Bristol Harbor. The house is constructed on an outcrop of ledge near the end of Hope Street, with its back to the street is not far from the boat yard. The house's isolation and the fact that it fronts Bristol Harbor are indicative of the attitude of its owner toward the public. He enjoys his privacy. His chief inspiration always came from the sea. His windows look far down Narragansett Bay, with Poppasquash Point stretching to the south and Prudence Island in the foreground. It is a picturesque bit of scenery, and as Capt. Nat had an interesting family, it is no wonder that he is satisfied with his home.

A certain Capt. Albert C. Bennett, a Bristol veteran of sixty-four ocean crossings in sailing vessels, sailed with the Herreshoffs, both father and son, a greater number of times, probably more, than any other one man. Capt. Bennett said he only saw Nat excited in a race once. It was in a race in Gowanus Bay, when the future designer of America's Cup defenders was at the helm. The breeze slackened, and it was thought advisable to raise a topsail, but in the course of this operation, one of the corners got away from the crew and the sail went flapping high into the air. Capt. Nat took off his cap, flung it down on the deck, and the language in which he indulged himself for a moment is said to have been extremely "forcible."

"But that's the only time," said Capt. Bennett, "that I ever saw him when he seemed to be excited." As the yachting alliance knows very well, Nat was uniformly cool and careful in a race, sailing his craft for "all she is worth," making few tactical errors.

On one occasion, he was steering the *Janthe* in a race near New York, when the breeze almost deserted the boats and left them idly moving in the direction of home, but at a snail's pace. There were two or more classes of yachts in the fleet, but the skipper of the *Janthe*, steering wide of his comrades ran into a little breeze he had seen far to starboard, and beat all the classes over the finish line. It is by such careful and cool-headed observation that opens possibilities to the wide-awake helmsman in every race that he won his great reputation as a sailor.

CAPT. NAT'S SUSPICION OF SPIES

Nat Herreshoff was known to be secretive and taciturn to point of paranoia. The following paragraphs accurately summarize one aspect of the personality of the most brilliant naval architect the America's Cup has never known.

For his entire life, he was haunted by a fear of having his ideas stolen, of being victimized by a spy. He posted armed guards at the boat sheds where his successful defenders were being built, in an effort to push away the curious and discourage intrusive photographers. His attitude is commonplace today; a quick walk around the Port America's Cup in Valencia, Spain where the 2007–Cup races were scheduled to play out would verify that, but for his time, it was extremely unusual and obsessive behavior.

Herreshoff, focused on his profession as an exclusive passion to the detriment of his close relations. After the death in 1891 of his friend Edward Burgess, who had designed three victorious defenders (*Puritan* in 1885, *Mayflower* in 1886 and *Volunteer* in 1887), Nat welcomed Burgess' son, William Starling, to Bristol for the holidays. The teenager spent hours watching his 'uncle' Nat carving his models.

Near the end of 1896, the young Burgess followed the construction of the *Sally II*, a small five-meter boat that had been conceived by Herreshoff as a gift for the boy's eighteenth birthday. During its construction, the teenager confided to Herreshoff his ambition to become a naval architect, like his father. Herreshoff's reaction was swift and harsh; he expelled Burgess from his workshop, banishing him from seeing any of his work in progress. This did not prevent Burgess from realizing his goal to become a designer. In fact, he would design Cup defenders three times between 1930 and 1937, including the J-class boats *Enterprise, Rainbow,* and with Olin Stephens, he designed the *Ranger.*

The "Wizard of Bristol" was not discriminatory in his paranoia. He had the same reaction to his own son, L. Francis, who was also very interested in his father's work. Aggravated, Nat sent his son to the Rhode Island State Agricultural School, which today is the University of Rhode Island. L. Francis settled into his work as a farmer before becoming a renowned designer who created the unsuccessful defense candidate in the 1930–Cup defense, the J-class *Whirlwind.*

Capt. Nat had a fear of spies for his entire working life and lived in constant suspicion of people stealing his ideas. However, he did inspire an entire generation of designers. Although he was not a victim of any obvious act of espionage, his paranoia also inspired the suspicion that hovers over Cup secrecy to this day.

A CUP DEFENDER CONTRACT

The Herreshoff Manufacturing Company of this town has received an order, given by a New York Syndicate, for a steel boat of the required size, as a defender of the America's Cup and will soon commence its construction.

Mr. J. B. Herreshoff is quoted as saying, "The Company has contracted to build a Cup defender, The contract is made with Mr. Archibald Rogers of New York as the head of the syndicate. We do not know who the other gentlemen are, All our dealings have been with Mr. Rogers. The boat will be built of steel and set up in the same shop soon as the Carroll 84-footer can be got out of the way. The material is contracted for some of it will be here next week, and all of it within a fortnight.

In view of the importance of the contest for the Cup, and the need of keeping as much as possible about it secret until the challenger is under way, I trust you will see the impossibility of my giving further information about the boat. She is ordered and we will build her as fast as we can build her."

Mr. Oliver Iselin, the former owner of the crack sloop *Titania*, says, "The Herreshoffs are, without doubt, the leading yacht designers in this country and they will undoubtedly turn out a boat fast enough to keep the Cup, so I fail to see the necessity of another boat. A Cup defender would probably cost about $75.000, which would make it an expensive plaything for one season."

Bristol Phoenix December 24, 1892.

THE *COLONIA*

Monday evening a few minutes after seven o'clock, the first of the four America-Cup defenders, bearing the name *Colonia*, was successfully launched from the Herreshoff Company's Yard in this town. There was only a small gathering of spectators to witness the launching as no public announcement had been made and the affair was without ceremony.

The *Colonia* is said to be the largest sloop ever built in this country. She is 126 feet overall, and the length of the water line 85 feet, draft about 16 feet. She is painted white with green underneath; she is a handsome vessel. The riggers commenced their labors Monday morning.

Bristol Phoenix May 20, 1893.

THE *COLONIA'S* TRIAL TRIP

The *Colonia*, the yacht built by the Herreshoffs for the Rogers syndicate, made a trial trip Monday; the wind was unfavorable but it was plainly demonstrated that she will be a very fast sailor.

Bristol Phoenix June 17, 1893.

THE *VIGILANT* LEAVES BRISTOL

The Cup defender *Vigilant*, built by the Herreshoff Mfg. Co., sailed for New York last Tuesday night, having her owners and friends on board, it is expected that the vessel will make a fine record, and if chosen to defend America's Cup will get there.

Bristol Phoenix July 22, 1893.

THE *VIGILANT*

The challenge of the *Valkyrie II* for 1893, brought out three new boats to try out for the privilege of defending the Cup, they were the *Vigilant*, the *Colonia*, and the *Pilgrim*. The first two were built by the Herreshoffs, and the last one by a Boston firm. The *Vigilant* was a centerboard, the *Colonia* a keel craft; the struggle to be declared the defender was confined to these two, which had the same upper-body type as the *Gloriana*. The Boston boat could not keep pace with the Bristol boats. The *Volunteer* which had been changed to a schooner and re-rigged as a sloop, to act as a "trial horse," made a poor showing alongside Capt. Nat's creations.

The *Vigilant*, built of Tobin bronze, for strength and lightness showed her to be the better all-round boat and was selected as the defender of the Cup. The *Viligant's* principal dimensions were: overall length, 126 feet; waterline, 86.2; beam, 26; draft, 13.3; sail area, 11, 272 square feet.

The *Valkyrie II*, like the *Thistle*, was designed by George L. Watson, one of England's foremost yacht designers, with especial view to meeting the conditions of American waters. She was an advancement of the *Thistle* model, in other words, a wider departure from the old English cutter type, while the appearance of her bow indicated that the good points of the *Gloriana* had not been entirely overlooked by her designer. She was only nine inches shorter on the water line than the *Vigilant* and she carried 1,230 square feet less sail.

In all previous matches, the superiority was on the side of the defender. Three races were sailed and the *Vigilant* easily won the first and second, by 5 minutes 48 seconds, and 10 minutes 35 seconds respectively after allowing the *Valkyrie II* 1 minute 48 seconds. The third race was also won, but by the narrow margin of 40 seconds.

The following editorials taken from the *Bristol Phoenix* of 1893 are testimony to the Herreshoffs' success in racing yacht design.

> The *Vigilant's* success is Bristol's, for this is the birthplace of the yacht that outsails the world and brings fame to her designers. "Nat Herreshoff won't give a fellow a chance to win" was the disgusted comment of one of Capt. Nat's old-time adversaries. Our amiable and sportsmanlike visitor Lord Dunraven probably feels about that way himself.
>
> New York [Yacht Club] is boasting now of her first victory in the international contest since *Genesia* came over. For it was a Boston boat that beat *Genesia* and a Boston boat that beat *Thistle*—The New York boats (for those races) were built in New York.
>
> This year New York came to Bristol for a boat and the result was *Vigilant* and *Colonia* two of the dandiest flyers that the world has ever known. The *Phoenix* rises to remark that it is proud of the fact that it hails from the same town as Nat Herreshoff.
>
> *Bristol Phoenix* Oct. 21, 1893

THE *VIGILANT* BATTLES ON

> It matters not as to whether the *Vigilant*, in which our citizens take so much interest, be a winner or loser in the number of races over the other side of the water, it will not detract from the splendid victories heretofore won by the Herreshoffs in the numerous races in which the English sportsmen have met their crack yachts and been defeated.

Yet it must be recollected that although the Herreshoffs are the builders of the *Vigilant*, she is owned by a gentleman who never was a true sportsman. It is [Jay] Gould, the owner, who is the loser or winner. Let the Prince of Wales bring the *Britannia* to Newport next season and if there is not more than an even score in the settlement won by the Yankees in their own waters, then they will settle down to the fact that "Britannia rules the waves," but not until then. There is no doubt that the *Vigilant* has been handicapped in every way and it is doubtful if she is in as fine a racing trim as she was last season. Then taking into consideration the perfect understanding they have of the tides that prevail in those waters, it must be conceded that there is a chance of her being beaten by an English skipper whose experience is unquestioned.

Bristol Phoenix July 28, 1894

THAT *VIGILANT* AGAIN

The last few races of the *Vigilant* seem to have proved satisfactory to the average Bristolian, that in an open sea with equal chances, the *Britannia* is no match for her, provided there is wind enough to fill her canvass, and with the fair-minded English sportsman she is rated as being the fastest boat of her kind in [her home] waters.

It is not a wonder that they rate Mr. Herreshoff as the greatest designer in the yacht building line in the world. A *New York Herald* correspondent gives an interview with a prominent member of the Royal Victoria Yacht Club as follows:

I look upon it that the *Vigilant* is a wonderfully designed boat, for she travels better on her side than she does on a level keel. She does not stand up to the wind like the *Britannia*, and that very lack of stiffness seems to favor her, for the further she heels the faster she seems to go. In fact, she never appears to get her full way on until she is well over on her side. I look upon it that her bronze bottom, which is like the glass of a watch, is of great advantage to her. If I were going to order a boat to beat the world, I would go to Mr. Herreshoff.

Bristol Phoenix Aug. 11, 1894

THE *VIGILANT* RETURNS TO BRISTOL

[The] *Vigilant*, the ex-Cup defender, arrived in Bristol early Saturday morning. She was towed into the harbor by the tug *Aeronaut* from New York. It is her first appearance in these waters in two years. Capt. Charles Barr is skipper of the *Vigilant* and he is on board in command. She has a crew of 30 men and 10 or 12 more are engaged which will make the full complement needed during the season. Her object in coming to Bristol now is to procure a centerboard, and yesterday morning she was towed out into the ship channel and anchored just north of Castle Island beacon in Bristol Harbor for the purpose of having the new center board hung.

Bristol Phoenix June 11, 1895.

CONTRACTING THE *DEFENDER*

When Lord Dunraven issued another challenge for 1895, New York Yacht Club members C. Oliver Iselin, William K. Vanderbilt, and E. D. Morgan, who had been members of the syndicate, which built the *Vigilant*, commissioned the Herreshoffs to build them a new boat called *Defender*.

Bristol Phoenix 1893

BUILDING THE *DEFENDER*

While the new yacht *Defender* has been in process of construction at Bristol, Rhode Island, public attention has been attracted in no small measure to that town and to the man who has designed and built the craft. It is only a few years ago that Edward Burgess was regarded as the greatest yacht designer of the day; and when he died, in 1891; the prediction was freely made that his equal would not soon be developed. Other men might be found who would design fast yachts, but the chances were that if the British yachtsmen should challenge for the *America's* trophy again, the Cup would presently be on its way to the other side of the ocean. At least that was the conclusion at which a great many pessimistic observers arrived when they learned of the untimely death of the man who had created the *Puritan*, the *Mayflower*, and the *Volunteer*. But almost at the moment of Mr. Burgess's death the victories of the *Gloriana* were pointing unmistakably to Nat Herreshoff as the designer upon whom the task of producing another international champion might profitably be imposed.

Bristol Phoenix, 1895

SAILS FOR THE *DEFENDER*

The sails of the new Cup defender, which will be laid down in the large unoccupied room at the rubber works will be made of ramie cloth, a material manufactured from grasses that grow in Texas, and also in eastern countries. It is much lighter and tougher than cotton or linen duck and when wet is even stronger than when dry. In color, the cloth is nearly white, shading a trifle on the yellow. The reporters of the metropolitan press will now have another place to storm but much good it will do them, for the room used in making the sails will be as carefully guarded as is the Herreshoff Works.

Bristol Phoenix March 26, 1895.

TUNING THE *DEFENDER*

[The] *Defender* and *Colonia* sailed up from Newport yesterday and dropped anchor off Herreshoff's about two o'clock. *Defender's* trial with *Vigilant* off Newport Sunday demonstrated that *Defender* is much faster than the old champion is, and everybody is satisfied that the new racer will be a winner. *Defender* will be finished up, turned over to the syndicate, and taken to New York in time for the big races there off Sandy Hook on Saturday and Monday.

Bristol Phoenix July 19, 1895

The following narrative describing the *Defender's* attributes is from the September 1895 issue of *Munsey's Magazine* by an anonymous author:

Like a great white cloud coming on the wind, or some wonderful bird from the regions of snow, *Defender* sailed down the sound from her cradle at Bristol, proud, graceful, and confident. It was the confidence of her superiority she seemed to show, a confidence in the magic of her lines and the might of her white sails, a proud certainty that she could out sail all that had gone before her, and, above all, a pride in the knowledge that upon her depended the honor of American yachting, that made *Defender* seem all but human, and impressed those who beheld her with the feeling that she was built to win.

Designed and constructed by the Herreshoffs, a firm of American yacht builders famous for the records their boats have always made, under the personal supervision of men whose yachting experience in the defense of the Cup had made them familiar with the defects of the past, and on the order of a syndicate which set no money limit, *Defender* has come to her task the perfect embodiment of all that experience, thought, and money can make a boat—as perfect a racing machine as ever left her cradle.

Yachting today comes so near flying that the development of the sport may, after all, be the initiative step in the art of navigating the air. It is this theory that the Herreshoffs had in mind when they designed *Defender*. The idea was to get the least resistance and give the greatest power, to hold as little as possible to the water and take as much as possible to the air. For a boat of her size *Defender* resists the water less than any craft afloat. The chief characteristic of the American boat, heretofore, the centerboard, has been abandoned that the hull might have its weight on its keel—which the fin prevented. Above the keel the task has been to secure buoyancy; but at the edge of the water the art of yacht building seems to have given place to that of flying. Thousands of feet of canvas stretch up and out into the air like monster wings, the question *Defender* answers is: what is the greatest amount of canvas a boat can stand and yet keep the necessary running grip on the water? So skillfully has this problem been handled, that the whole yachting world is marveling at the expanse of canvas the yacht is able to spread—between twelve and thirteen thousand square feet.

Since *Defender's* first trials it has been evident to her sailing masters, the only ones at all fit to judge, that in light winds she was a much faster boat than the last defender of the Cup, *Vigilant*. Her general work has not been altogether satisfactory to those who know of her powers only through what they read. She was expected to sail away from *Vigilant* easily, and she defeated the [Jay] Gould boat with but a narrow margin. It is the light wind; however that she will probably have to sail under in the race, and a light wind boat that she will have to meet.

In the *Defender*, the Herreshoffs developed the fin keel. She was constructed of aluminum and bronze, two feet shorter than the *Vigilant*
overall, but two and three tenths feet longer on the waterline, had about
three feet less beam and six feet more draft. During trials against the
Vigilant, she showed from the beginning superiority on every point of
sailing, and was chosen to meet the British new comer, *Valkyrie III*.

Watson had designed the *Valkyrie III*, like her predecessors in the last
two matches. She was a much larger and more powerful vessel than her
namesake in the 1893 race, and her sail area was even greater than that of
the *Defender*. Thus, the two nations had very nearly reached the common
type to which they had for almost a decade been approaching.

Returning to the September 1895 issue of *Munsey's Magazine* narrative,
this is what the contemporary author thought of the *Valkyrie III*.

> Lord Dunraven, in making a final attempt to recover the Queen's [America's]
> Cup, has endeavored, in *Valkyrie III*, to show how much he has learned from the
> defeat he suffered at the hand of *Vigilant* two years ago. In design and build his
> boat has had of English skill and general experience all that *Defender* claimed
> from America. Mr. [George L.] Watson, her maker, sailed with *Valkyrie II* when
> she raced *Vigilant*, and knew what was wanted, and what was expected of the
> new boat. For light winds, he has undoubtedly produced the fastest boat ever
> built in England. *Valkyrie III* showed this clearly in the run of June 29 with *Bri-
> tannia* and *Ailsa* at Rothesay, and again on the 15th of July in a run and reach of
> thirteen miles, in which she came in ten minutes ahead of the same competitors.
>
> After his defeat here in 1893, Dunraven made the remark that *Valkyrie*
> was no drifter, the accepted lesson of that defeat explains the character of
> the new challenger, and clears the mystery of her wonderful sailing in light
> winds. Certain it was that after the third race with *Vigilant* the English lord
> had the drifting speed of a boat well in mind, and in his molding of another
> *Valkyrie* challenger Watson doubtless gave the matter serious thought. Experts
> assert that it is this that gives *Valkyrie III* her great grace and beauty; but
> they express fear that she may be too tender a craft to stand up to her task
> of carrying her sails in a strong wind.
>
> Yachting men on the Clyde seem to place no great amount of confidence
> in *Valkyrie III*. The most they say is that she has a fair chance. Some condemn
> her wholly because she shows a few lines that are unmistakably American.

A glimpse of the models of the two racers reveals in each a singular imitation on the part of the designers—a delicate exchange of compliments, perhaps. Herreshoff has imitated the *Valkyrie II*; Watson has taken many of the lines of *Vigilant*. In the last Cup race both of these yacht makers saw good points in the rival boat, and each builder took advantage of what he saw.

The best that has been said of *Valkyrie III* was the expression made by Mr. Watson, when he remarked, "She satisfies me."

A gaggle of tongue-wagging yachtsmen feared the *Defender* to be quite unseaworthy; they worried that her mast would drop through her bottom during the races.

THE *DEFENDER* CAPTURES THE CUP

America's Cup is safe for at least another year, but the fiasco, which brings about the result, is very unsatisfactory to all true sportsmen. *Defender* squarely won Saturday's race. Tuesday's race was awarded *Defender* on a foul, after she had virtually won it by plainly showing her superiority over the Englishman, even in a crippled condition. In yesterday's race, Lord Dunraven withdrew *Valkyrie* immediately after the start. *Defender* went over the course alone and was awarded three races and the Cup.

Lord Dunraven does not claim that he was treated unfairly, but says he withdrew because of interference by the fleet of excursion steamers. He has laid himself open to the charge of not being a "dead game sport" and of being afraid of a crushing defeat yesterday in a strong breeze.

However, the Cup would have stayed here had three genuine races been sailed, *Defender's* corrected time over the 30-mile course yesterday, sailing alone without special effort, 4 hours, 43 minutes, and 43 seconds, which is fast under the circumstances. Mr. N. G. Herreshoff arrived in Bristol this morning and has expressed himself disgusted with the fizzle. He naturally wanted to know just how badly *Defender* could beat *Valkyrie*.

Bristol Phoenix September 13, 1895.

The essential differences between the two boats are shown by the following figures, those of the *Defender*: overall length, 124 feet; waterline,

88.5 feet; beam, 23.3; draft, 19; sail area, 12,650 square feet; *the Valkyrie III* measured thus: overall length, 125 feet; waterline, 88.85; beam, 23; draft, 16; and sail area, 13,028 square feet.

When the boats were measured, it was found that, for the first time in the struggles between "single-stickers," time allowance had to be given by the challenger to the defender. As 30-mile races were agreed on, the *Valkyrie III* allowed 29 seconds. The first race, sailed in a light breeze over a moderate ground swell, showed the superiority, both on and off the wind, of the *Defender*, which won by the comfortable margin of 8 minutes 49 seconds, corrected time. In the second encounter the *Defender*, although crippled immediately before the start by a deliberate foul, and thereby compelled to carry less canvas than her adversary, sailed a magnificent race, actually beating the *Valkyrie III*, over two-thirds of the course, and finishing only 1 minute 16 seconds behind—on corrected time, 47 seconds. *Defender's* owner Mr. C. O. Iselin protested the foul, and the committee gave the win to the *Defender*, which the circumstances warranted.

Lord Dunraven then withdrew from the match and sailed home in a huff.

THE *DEFENDER* RETURNS TO BRISTOL

The *Defender* will be put in first class shape for the trial races. Capt. John Terry of Fall River, with his workers, pile driver and other paraphernalia, arrived here Tuesday afternoon for the purpose of extending the ways at the Herreshoff shops out into the harbor a distance of about 290 feet. The work was begun Wednesday and is to be completed as soon as possible, so that *Defender*, which is now at Glen Island [New York], may be brought here and completely overhauled and put in good shape as a trial horse for the defense of the [America's] Cup.

The ways that were put down to launch *Defender* upon were taken up some time ago, and new ways will be put down nearly the entire length of 290 feet from the west end of the south construction shop. The distance beyond the end of where the ways were located for the launching of *Defender* is about 140 feet.

The *Defender's* topsides will be removed, and it is understood that a thicker plating of aluminum will replace the plating now on, the present aluminum plating being more or less corroded.

New deck beams of aluminum will also be substituted for the beams now in this yacht, which are of aluminum, and which are also corroded. The work of overhauling the *Defender* will be a long and slow job, and it is expected that the yacht will not be ready to go overboard until well into the spring.

Bristol Phoenix, 1898

THE *DEFENDER* SAFELY HOUSED

We learn of the reconstruction of Herreshoff's 1895 champion yacht the *Defender* from an undated 1902 *Bristol Phoenix* clipping.

The champion yacht *Defender* now lives safely in the south shop at Herreshoff's where she was built in '95. The work of hauling her out and getting her into the shop was completed about 4 o'clock Tuesday afternoon. The big steel cradle in which she rests is very strongly built. It moves on 30 iron wheels, each of which weighs 150 pounds. More than 30 men were employed to drawing *Defender* out. Now that the big yacht is under cover, the work of removing some of her plating above the water line for inspection has been going on, and will be continued until critical examination has been made to determine how much corrosion there is and how much of the plating will have to be replaced by new aluminum.

Several workers were employed on the interior of *Defender* Wednesday putting zinc between the deck and the aluminum braces that run across the top of the yacht close to the deck for strengthening pieces. The zinc was put in between the braces by means of a squirt gun, after which the braces are screwed up. There is considerable corrosion where the zinc is being put in, and it is believed that it will arrest this, the corrosion not having advanced far enough to weaken the aluminum to any great extent.

Workmen are at present engaged in construction the mould for the big lead keel, which will be run as soon as the *Defender* is out of the shop.

During the past few days quite a number of former employees in both the wood and metal working departments have been engaged.

LIPTON'S FIRST CHALLENGE

Lipton's boat, the *Shamrock*, was William Fife-built, who turned out some of the fastest yachts in English waters. On our side, the Herreshoffs built a fast new boat for C. Oliver Iselin and Commodore J. Pierpont Morgan, the *Columbia*.

There were many rumors regarding the *Shamrock*. There was none more improbable than the statement that the English boat was to carry a centerboard. The fate of the centerboard, as far as big yachts were concerned, was determined in 1893, when the keel boat *Valkyrie II* easily vanquished the centerboard *Vigilant* in a fifteen-mile rush to windward, against a stiff breeze. The *Valkyrie II* was the first of the ninety-footers to be built upon the fin-keel principle, just as the *Vigilant* was the last of the ninety-footers to carry a centerboard.

In 1895 the Herreshoffs abandoned the centerboard in favor of the fixed keel, the *Defender* was the first keel single-stick yacht built for the defense of the Cup. Therefore, it was not likely that Fife would return to a form of construction that had been abandoned by the people who so long used it and so thoroughly understood its possibilities.

According to the *Scientific American* dated July 8, 1899:

> On the subject of keels and centerboards, it is satisfactory to know that the *Columbia*, in the few trials which she had with the *Defender*, had shown, even before she had time to be "tuned up," that she was a somewhat faster boat. The difference was not remarkable, but it was obvious, and those who may have felt disappointed that she had not shown a more marked superiority must surely had remembered that was more difficult to make a gain of five minutes over a thirty-mile course in the present era [1899] of yacht designing than it was to make one of fifteen or twenty minutes a dozen years earlier. In competitive trials between the new and old Cup-defenders we must remember that *Defender* was a phenomenally fast boat. Now, *Columbia* will probably have about five minutes advantage of *Defender* on a thirty-mile course, and therefore, be taken to be from twenty to twenty-five minutes better than the last Fife ninety-foot yacht.

The *Shamrock*, the sixth British cutter seeking to capture the America's Cup was making her way across the Atlantic when the weekly *Scientific*

American newspaper dated August 12, 1899, wrote of the interest to compare this new challenger's sailing qualities against previous British yachts that made the same quest:

> It is a right royal line with which this Anglo-Scotch-Irish craft is associated in holding her title of challenger; and with her Irish name, Scotch design, and English construction, she is truly representative of the people to whose fostering care the early growth of the sport of yacht sailing and its present popularity are largely due.
>
> In the dimensions and construction of both defender and challenger, there was great similarity. The *Columbia*, though stronger than the *Defender*, was a remarkably light craft, and in the *Shamrock*, Thorneycroft with his quarter of a century experience building torpedo boats, produced a hull and spars that were probably an advance over Herreshoff's boat in the matter of light scantling up-to-the-limit construction. *Shamrock's* builders kept the boat's underwater shape shrouded in secrecy, no doubt endeavoring to conceal her excessive draught; wise observers suggested it not unlikely that she would be found to draw as much as 22 feet. This would mean lower lead, less of it, and a nearer approach to the true fin keel than had been shown in any 90-foot yacht since the construction of the *Pilgrim* in 1893.
>
> A study of the two vessels [reveal] notable differences in their sail plans. *Shamrock's* mast appears to be stepped about 2 feet further aft than *Columbia's*, and her bowsprit is considerably longer, the distance from mast to outer end of bowsprit being from 5 to 7 feet greater in *Shamrock*. Her present boom is about the same length as *Columbia's*. The gaff, topmast, and hoist of mainsail, on the other hand, are a few feet less than *Columbia's*, so that the sail plan is longer on the base line, but not as lofty as that of the American boat. She probably carries a larger spinnaker, larger headsails, and a similar mainsail, the effect of which, other things being equal, should be to give *Columbia* the advantage in windward work and *Shamrock* in reaching and running. Her owner, Sir Thomas Lipton, and her designer, "Willie" Fife, have both stated that she is to carry a larger mainsail in the races on this side.

The first race took place on October 3, in the presence of the largest spectator fleet yet assembled. Neither Lipton nor Morgan sailed aboard their racing yachts; rather, they enjoyed the spectacle from their palatial steam yachts.

THE *COLUMBIA* 1899

It is always interesting to read contemporary period publications' observations of notable events recorded soon after their occurrence. Here is
the description of the launching of the *Columbia*, from the *American
Monthly Review of Reviews*, July 1899.

> At a quarter past eight on the evening of June 10, Mrs. C. Oliver Iselin broke a
> bottle of champagne over the prow of the new Cup defender in the Herreshoff
> yards at Bristol. "I christen thee *Columbia* and I wish thee luck," said she.
>
> Simultaneous with the crash of shattered glass the beautiful bronze, with
> her under body gleaming like gold and her top sails glistening white, began
> to move slowly toward the water as the gigantic windlass attached to the
> steel cradle on which she was built revolved.
>
> With the first sign of motion came lusty cheers from 5,000 throats,
> ear-piercing shrieks from strident whistles, and salutes from yacht cannon.
> The scene was spectacular. It was rendered more theatric still because of
> the powerful calcium lights flashed on the shapely hull from the tender St.
> Michael.
>
> As the *Columbia* emerged from the shed Capt. Charles Barr, who with
> Nat Herreshoff and half a dozen sailors was on her deck, erected a flag-staff
> and broke out an immense silken yacht ensign. A few moments later, the
> private signals of her owners, Commodore Morgan and Mr. Iselin, were
> displayed from a jury-mast stepped in the aperture for the immense spar
> of Oregon pine which is to be placed in position immediately. The darkness
> of the night was made brilliant by the flash-lights of photographers and the
> glare of search-lights, all aimed at the hull of white and gold moving with
> grace and dignity to its baptism of seawater. Seventeen minutes elapsed
> before the stately fabric floated clear of the cradle and danced buoyantly in
> the element she is destined to adorn.
>
> A yachtsman of even ten years ago [1888] who had not kept up with the
> course of events in the '90s would not be a little astonished at the *Columbia*.
> She is of the fin-keel type (that queer modern shape whose name is very
> descriptive and which gives her, with a beam of 24 feet, no less than 20
> feet draught), and to the uninitiated she is hardly to be distinguished from
> *Defender*. The experts pick her out by minute differences in spreaders,

counter, nose and gaff topsail, quite invisible to an untrained eye. In reality she exhibits the other boat's characteristic features in an even more marked degree, having a still longer overhang forward and aft (the particular improvement introduced by the Herreshoffs), a greater cutting away of the fore-foot, still more rake in the stern-post, a flatter floor, deeper draught, smaller wetted surface, and more sail area.

A few figures will give an idea of what a peculiar racing machine had been evolved by modern competition. With a total length of 131 feet, *Columbia's* load water-line measures only 89 feet 6 inches; that is to say, one-third of her length is "in the air" as receding bow and overhanging stern. Her "backbone" is an inch thick bronze keel-plate, reinforced by three inches of flanges and cross-webs, so that there is in effect four inches of metal to carry, below, the great lead keel weighing 90 tons; above, the floors and frames of the vessel. The huge stick of Oregon pine first used as a mast was 107½ feet long and weighed about 4 tons. At this writing [1899] it is being replaced by a steel mast a few inches shorter and tapering both ways from a center diameter of 22¼ inches. This will take off fully a ton of weight above the deck and is expected to make the boat much stiffer in the wind. Her topmast is 68 feet long, bowsprit 38, spinnaker 73, and she can carry sails aggregating 13,500 square feet—nearly 1,000 more than *Defender*.

The author of this *American Monthly Review of Reviews* essay goes on with several more facts that are interesting. The professional American crew of 34 sailors, four quartermasters, and a second mate, all hailed from Deer Island, Maine, owner C. Oliver Iselin managed them and sailing master Scotsman Charlie Barr, who had sailed the *Minerva* and the *Colonia* to victory in nearly every race, which they were entered. The crew earned $45 a month and an additional $4 for each race. It is assumed the crew was promised a healthy-sized bonus if the *Columbia* successfully defended the Cup. It is further assumed that the wealthy gentlemen who supplied this defender probably shelled-out well over $250,000 toward the effort.

The *Columbia*, Nat Herreshoff's masterpiece of beauty and speed, successful defender of the Cup in the 1899 match, was selected once again to meet the challenger in the 1901 match. Although this would seem to be a precedent setting decision, it was the only time that the same yacht defended the Cup in two consecutive races until1967 and 1970 when the

The 1901 Cup Defender contender the *Independence* was considered by many the fastest boat to defend the America's Cup, but she proved to be too fragile and was dismissed after a dismal showing in trial races.

Intrepid was the defender, and in 1974 and 1977 when the *Courageous* defended the Cup. Both of these yachts were the designs of Olin J. Stephens.

The run up to the selection of the *Columbia* as defender consisted of match races between Herreshoff-built *Columbia,* and *Constitution*, and Boston-built *Independence*.

B.B. Crowninshield who belonged to a family long involved in Salem shipping designed the Independence. Popular thought in Boston was the new yacht could easily beat all the New York boats as General Paine had with the *Puritan, Mayflower*, and *Volunteer*. As it turned out, the designer had all the troubles that he imagined because the hull, and spars, rigging, fittings and sails were all built by separate companies and came together as pieces in a jigsaw puzzle.

In his 1963 book, *An Introduction to Yachting*, L. Francis Herreshoff relates his personal observation of the *Independence*:

> I must say that when I saw the picture of the *Independence* I thought my father's Cup boats would be beaten by *Independence*, but things turned out quite differently for she had structural trouble and leaked badly; she did not steer well, and her very flat model had so much wetted surface that she was very dull in light weather.

The other new Cup boat for 1901 was *Constitution* built for a syndicate of New York Yacht Club members headed by August Belmont. She was designed by Mr. [Nat] Herreshoff and managed by William Butler Duncan who had run

Defender when she was the trial boat for *Columbia* in 1899. In model and sail plan *Constitution* was an enlarged *Columbia* but her construction was quite novel for she was the first vessel built on what is called longitudinal framing over widely spaced web frames, a construction that has the advantages of:

- greater strength for its weight,
- plating can be laid flush with one of the longitudinal frames making a continuous butt strap at the seams,
- local strains, such as the mast step, *et cetera*, can be taken care of by the location of the web frames,
- this type of framing, when properly designed, is the cheapest.

THE *COLUMBIA* 1901

A new syndicate was formed to meet Lipton's 1901 challenge, and again Herreshoff received the contract for a defender, the new boat was the *Constitution*. She was as large as the *Shamrock II* and carried about 200 square feet more sail than Lipton's boat.

During that summer there arose a great competition to choose the yacht to defend the Cup. Naturally, the New York Yacht Club syndicate expected its candidate would receive the honor. Club member Mr. E. D. Morgan bought Oliver Iselin's share of the *Columbia* and entered that old defender in the trials.

Word came out of Boston that wealthy stockbroker Thomas W. Lawson was building a defender—a big sloop called *Independence*.

Lawson was not part of the New York Yacht Club's alliance, therefore he was informed he would have to join the Club or put his potential defender in the name of a member if he wanted to join the Cup trials. Stubbornly, Lawson refused to do either.

The *Columbia's* owners J. Pierpont Morgan and Edwin D. Morgan had their 1899 Cup defender refitted, and enlisted Skipper Charlie Barr to return to the helm of the boat, which he had steered, to victory against the *Shamrock* two years earlier.

In the heat of the summer trial races *Columbia* and *Constitution* met several times and *Columbia* out sailed her rival.

The *Columbia*, a fin keel sloop, designed and built in 1898 by Nathanael G. Herreshoff for owners J. Pierpont Morgan and Edwin Dennison Morgan of the New York Yacht Club, successfully defended the Cup in 1899 and 1901.

Late in the summer the *Independence* showed up to join in the trials. She surprised the gathered Corinthians for her radical design, which was of a racing scow; with a huge sail spread, predicted as cumbersome in anything but the most favorable weather conditions. As a courtesy, the Newport Yacht Racing Association scheduled some races for the new boat to show her strengths. In these matches the *Independence* always finished last, which put an end to Lawson's defender bid.

During the trial races, observers were surprised by the strong performance of *Columbia*. A sport writer for the *New York Tribune* wrote of the July 2, 1901 race:

> Barr was crouching over his wheel and sailing *Columbia* fine, some said too fine, but Barr knows his boat and he was now steering for his future and his reputation.
>
> It is important to add that he was in perfect symbiosis with his Scandinavian crew. The sail trim was always perfect, the spinnaker was hoisted in

less time than the others, and the boat slipped around the marks as if she were a catboat!

Fascinated by Charlie Barr's talent, the famous American historian W. P. Stephens wrote that the ex-Scotsman "handled *Columbia* as a man would a bicycle." Certainly, he had the slower sailboat, but he made life hard for Rhodes and as Thomas F. Day observed, "Barr simply made a monkey of the other man … forcing him to do whatever he wished."

According to L. Francis Herreshoff, *Columbia* and *Constitution* met twenty times during that summer. Each yacht won nine of the meets and two races were called off for lack of wind. Later in that season of trials, *Columbia* won regularly. Because the two yachts were so evenly matched, the win went to whoever got the start. The Cup Committee made the decision to choose the *Columbia* to meet the *Shamrock II*.

Early on the morning of October 4, the day of the third and final race, Captain Barr and sail maker, Mr. Hathaway from the Herreshoff sail loft, attempted to shorten the head rope of the *Columbia's* mainsail. *Columbia's* sails were old and had stretched out considerably and the head of the mainsail was now longer than the gaff.

The *Columbia* beat the *Shamrock II* in all three meets. The first race on September 28 was a 30-mile windward-leeward course that *Columbia* won by 1 minute 20 seconds corrected time. The second race took place on October 3 on a 30-mile triangular course; *Columbia* beat *Shamrock II* by 3 minutes 45 seconds corrected time. The third race took place on October 4 over a 40-mile windward-leeward course that the *Columbia* won by 41 seconds corrected time; actually, the *Shamrock II* had beaten *Columbia* by 2 seconds, elapsed time.

THE *RELIANCE* 1903

Launching the *Reliance* as reported in the April 10, 1903 issue of the *Bristol Phoenix*.

Herreshoff launched the latest America's Cup defender, one of the most famous boats to defend the Cup.

Seen racing on August 25, 1903, the *Reliance* the largest of all America's Cup defenders is Capt. Nat's greatest triumph. She was the most powerful and complex racing sloop in the world. Stereo view card image.

Reliance, the sixth yacht built by the Herreshoff Manufacturing Co., as a Cup defender, was successfully launched Saturday evening from the south shop, whence all but one of the six has emerged to take their maiden dip in the [Bristol] harbor.

The launching was witnessed by many thousand spectators, who lined Hope Street from the Lawless pier south to Walley Street. On the slope of the grounds of ex-Gov. A. O. Bourn, north of Walley Street, a large crowd gathered to witness the event in which many nations were interested.

On the north pier of the shops there was a large gathering of people mostly employees of the shop and their families. The members of the Rhode Island Automobile Club and friends viewed the launching from this point. In the south shop the invited guests, who included members of the press viewed the new racer to their heart's content from bow to stern and from deck to keel. Most of those in the south shop went to the south pier after the yacht had left the shop.

The launching of the *Reliance* in daylight was a great attraction for those who had cameras and the yacht as it slowly moved down the railway had hundreds of them pointed at her from every direction. The pictures were for biograph machines to be reproduced in theatres.

The big yacht filled the whole shop above the floor and looked every inch a racer as she stood in the cradle, seemingly waiting for the word to go.

Miss Iselin appeared to be a trifle nervous as she stepped on the platform which came out from the gallery to the starboard bow of the yacht. She was handed a hammer made especially for the occasion, the hammer being of silver and the handle of mahogany.

It was 5:28 o'clock when N. G. Herreshoff rang the gong for the starting of the engine and drum which was to lower away the cradle and its precious burden. Engineer J. T. Robertson immediately started the engine and just as the bow moved, Miss Iselin struck the bottle of champagne with the hammer. It was shivered into many small pieces and the contents sprayed over the side of the bow, on Miss Iselin's dress and fell on the floor of the shop. As the hammer staruck the bottle Miss Iselin said: "I name thee *Reliance*. Speed on to victory." The pieces of the bottle were quickly picked up as souvenirs by many of those near them.

The *Reliance*, reputed to be the largest and fastest Cup defender ever built, was certainly a masterpiece and the thoroughbred of the genre.

Masterminding the New York Yacht Club's effort to retain the Cup was the scientific-minded Capt. Nat; he, an innovative designer and engineer who had created three previous Cup defenders—each different than the other. When the *Reliance* emerged from the Herreshoff Manufacturing Co. construction shed into Bristol Harbor, in the words of the report of the local newspaper, "Loud and boisterous cheers filled the air."

In the minds of seasoned yachtsmen, The *Reliance* was a "skimming dish," a flat-bottomed, shallow-draft hull modeled on inland racing scows; of course including a few key Herreshoff modifications for sailing in rough weather.

Under the measurement rule governing the series, only the waterline length and sail area were computed to gauge the yacht's handicap. The two designers built yachts that were 90 feet on the waterline; both were longer if the bow and stern overhangs were counted. Each contender carried an enormous amount of sail; the *Shamrock III* carried 14,154 square feet, and the *Reliance* carried 16,159 square feet. For the *Reliance,* it was the largest sail plan ever set on a single-masted yacht; but in other elements of their designs, nearly opposite ideas prevailed. Fife, the challenger's designer, took a more traditional and conservative course, while Herreshoff's design was radical and experimental.

While the final trials for the honor of defending the Cup began on July thirtieth. To seasoned yachtsmen, it seemed almost certain that the *Reliance* would be chosen. She has shown up superbly in almost every sort of sea, in light and strong winds alike. She has beaten by over twenty minutes the record for a windward and leeward course of thirty miles. Granted her superiority to *Constitution* and *Columbia*, it is, however, safe to say that this superiority is not as great as the recent race figures seem to show. She is better canvassed than the *Constitution*, and is managed by Captain Barr, while *Columbia* is sailed by an amateur—which makes a lot of difference. The *Reliance* is built, to a considerable extent, along the lines of Lawson's *Independence*. It is scow-shaped at both bow and stern, but does not pound the water in rough weather, as did the Boston boat. Her hull is broad and shallow, while that of *Shamrock III* is comparatively speaking, narrow and deep. The British yacht, like the *Reliance*, has a scow stern, but the bow is like the half of a cone that has been cut lengthwise.

The fact that the racing yachts carry so much canvas is not the result of chance or mere whim on the part of the designers. In the building of these yachts, the effect of every extra inch of sail has been calculated with mathematical exactness. Years of experience and a vast amount of experiment have proved that the light, more or less scow-shaped, and comparatively broad and shallow hull offers the least resistance to the water. The Herreshoffs adopted the English idea of very deep keels loaded with lead, which balance the weight of the gigantic masts and sails and the wind pressure against them. Strength, however, has been sacrificed to speed, and the towering steel masts of both *Reliance* and *Shamrock III* were broken early in the season.

L. Francis Herreshoff wrote the following about his father Capt. Nat:

At the time *Reliance* was designed her designer was fifty-four years old and perhaps at the peak of his genius. Even then, she would not have been possible if Mr. Herreshoff had not had his own very complete yacht building establishment and sail loft manned by a picked crew whom he had trained to be particularly skillful workers. The *Reliance* cost $175,000.00, but it is very doubtful if she could be duplicated for one million today [1963] for there was a lot of manual work on her—such as beautiful forgings and hand-finished castings that it would be nearly impossible to find people to make now.

THE *RESOLUTE* 1920

The planned 1914 Cup races were interrupted for twelve years because of the European war. This time span would seem to have advantaged the potential American defenders—allowing ample time to design, build, and tune their vessels. Three yachts were built to compete for the honor of defending the Cup, they were the *Defiance*, *Vanitie*, and *Resolute*; all were slightly under 75 feet waterline length.

The *Defiance* was the concept of George Owen, a professor of naval architecture at MIT, several subcontractors built her piece by piece; William Gardner designed the *Vanitie*, she was built by the George Lawley boat yard in Boston. The third contender, the *Resolute*, was the sixth Cup defender designed and built by Capt. Nat Herreshoff who enjoyed the great advantage of having his design built almost entirely in his own yard. L. Francis Herreshoff remarked:

> Mr. Herreshoff was sixty years old when *Resolute* was built, and seventy-two years old the year she defended the Cup.

The *New York Times* published this article dated April 25, 1914, concerning the launch of the *Resolute*.

> BRISTOL, R.I., April 24—The bronze sloop Yacht *Resolute*, with six present and past flag officers of the New York Yacht Club will offer as a defender of the America's Cup, is near enough to completion to warrant her being launched at sunset to-morrow [*sic*]. She will be rigged speedily and go into commission for her first trial sail probably in ten days, or about the time that the other two defenders are ready for launching.
>
> In recognition of their four months' work on the yacht, the draughtsmen, metalworkers, riveters, and riggers were guests at a dinner to-night [*sic*] by Robert W. Emmons, 2d, of Boston, the manager of the *Resolute*, representing the owners. Mr. Emmons formally thanked the workers.

The *Resolute* has been built for Vice Commodore George F. Baker, Jr., Rear Commodore J. P. Morgan, former Commodores F. G. Bourne, Cornelius Vanderbilt and A. C. James, and former Vice Commodore Henry Walters. Secretary George A. Cormack of the New York Yacht Club is secretary of the syndicate and will sail on the yacht with Mr. Emmons. Another amateur, Charles Francis Adams, 2d, Treasurer of Harvard College and one of the most experienced helmsmen on the coast will handle the boat.

The *Resolute* was laid down on Dec. 12, but work was suddenly stopped on the 20th on account, it was said, of a change in the plans. It was resumed six days later and has progressed steadily since then.

As in the case of the other Cup defense yachts constructed at the Herreshoff works, a great deal of secrecy regarding the plans has reviled. In line with this policy, the *Resolute* will be launched as were the *Columbia, Constitution,* and *Reliance,* in the fading twilight. As an additional precaution against revealing her lines, the *Resolute* will slide down greased ways like a battleship, instead of being lowered into the water in a cradle.

Her rating will be announced before the first races with the other defenders, in order that the time allowance may be reckoned, but her dimensions will be withheld. It is understood that the *Resolute* is an enlargement of the fifty-foot sloops, nine of which were built last year by the Herreshoffs for members of the New York Yacht Club.

It is reported that he *Resolute* is smaller than the other two-Cup candidates, and may obtain an allowance from the *Defiance* of five minutes in the thirty-mile race.

Consensus between competing yacht clubs on both sides of the Atlantic was about the need to make the competing boats less expensive and less complicated, and the racing more competitive, thereby opening the competition to yacht clubs with fewer wealthy members able to finance the design and construction of very expensive racers. It was at the urging of the New York Yacht Club that Capt. Nat devised the Universal Rule, the plan that took into consideration Sir Thomas' proposal to limit waterline length to 75 feet.

Until the 1920 series, competitors were not required to conform to an identical design formula and the contenders varied greatly in their measurements; therefore, handicaps were employed in an attempt to make the contestants equal. The 1920 contenders were built to Herreshoff's Universal Rule, attempting to make both challenger and defender uniform, seaworthy, and practical. However, there were still differences and time allowances were applied for the last time in the history of the matches.

Spectators at the 14th challenge for the America's Cup watched Lipton's *Shamrock IV* come to within a whisper of taking the Cup back to Britain. After losing the first two races to Lipton's racer, Capt. Nat, now 72 years old, was rushed to New York, he and skipper Charles Francis Adams worked feverishly making adjustments to *Resolute's* rig, which evidently unleashed the full potential of Capt. Nat's brilliant Cup defender. The *Resolute* lived up to her name and won the final three matches in the series of five races.

For Capt. Nat, 1920 marked the end of a 37-year winning streak where his innovative and graceful designs had kept the America's Cup safe in its New York Yacht Club home. As one of the yachting fraternity's most revered and inventive designers, Nathanael Greene Herreshoff left his unmistakable fingerprints on the marquee of sailing excellence. He designed more than 2,000 vessels propelled by steam power and by wind power. Adding to Capt. Nat's six Cup-winning designs, the Herreshoff Manufacturing Company built two additional defenders, one in 1930, and another in 1934.

THE *ENTERPRISE* 1930

The Herreshoff Manufacturing Company built the *Enterprise*, a 121-foot J-class sloop, designed by W. Starling Burgess when the boat yard was under the management of Bristol's Haffenreffer family. The 1930 Cup defender was Big! Owned by the Aldrich Syndicate, the *Enterprise* was 80 feet on the waterline with an overall length of 120 feet; she displaced 128 tons and carried 7,583 square feet of sail. The so-called Park Avenue boom was first used on the *Enterprise*. Her original spruce mast was replaced with a circular section double-skin duralumin mast; her hull was plated with Tobin bronze, and she pioneered the use of retractable spreaders. *Enterprise* easily won four straight races with Lipton's *Shamrock V*, thereby adding more laurels to the Herreshoff name.

THE *RAINBOW* 1934

In 1934, sooner than expected, Thomas O. M. Sopwith, an experienced British yachtsman, made a new challenge. He commissioned Charles E. Nicholson to design and build the *Endeavour.*

As with the Watson-designed *Shamrock II* in 1901, which was the first boat to be designed following numerous towing-tank tests, the William Starling Burgess-designed *Rainbow* was the first J to be conceived according to the same principles: during two months in 1931, at the tank-test facilities at the University of Michigan, dozens of models were tested by Burgess.

The *Rainbow*, a formable speedster was launched from the Herreshoff yards on May 15, 1934. Her hull was Tobin bronze below the waterline over steel frames and steel above the waterline; her mast was duralumin, boom and spinnaker wood; waterline length 82 feet, overall length 127 feet 7 inches, displacement 141 tons, and a sail spread of 7,535 square feet.

The challenger *Endeavor* was a faster boat than the defender. The *Endeavour* won the first two races in the best four of seven series, and she was ahead in the third race when she ran into calm air. Tactical errors kept her from winning that race and the three, which followed.

Superb sail handling by *Rainbow's* crew of 31, and expert strategy on the part of Skipper Harold Vanderbilt brought the *Rainbow* through to victory. The New York Yacht Club's 1934 Cup defender, winner of the 15th America's Cup challenge defeated *Endeavour* by four wins to two.

The owner syndicate organized by Harold S. Vanderbilt, was joined by these gentlemen of capital: Frederick W. Vanderbilt, William K. Vanderbilt, Alfred G. Vanderbilt, J. P. Morgan, Gerard B. Lambert, Marshall Field, Edward S. Harkness, George F. Baker, Jr., Charles Hayden, George E. Roosevelt, W. G. McCullough, Joseph P. Day, Henry H. Rogers, Walter P. Chrysler, Ogden L. Mills, Alfred P. Sloane, Jr., and Winthrop W. Aldrich.

After the 1934 America's Cup win, the *Rainbow* was laid up in dry dock for two years in Bristol, where Vanderbilt later refitted her for use as trial horse. She was sold to Chandler Hovey in 1937, to race the defender selection trials, but the *Ranger* eliminated her. *Rainbow* was again laid up at the end of 1937 at Herreshoff's Bristol yard and came to an ignominious end in 1940 when she was sold for scrap.

Sir Tom's first attempt to lift the Cup from the Yankees
came in 1899, in his sloop, the *Shamrock*.

CHAPTER EIGHT

The Shamrock Challengers (1899–1930)

THE 1899 MATCH

THE CHALLENGE OF SIR Thomas Lipton, for the 1899 match revived good international feelings. Lipton's boat, the *Shamrock*, was William Fife-built, Watson's principal competitor, who turned out some of the fastest yachts in English waters. On our side, the Herreshoffs built a fast new boat for C. Oliver Iselin and Commodore J. Pierpont Morgan, the *Columbia*.

According to the *Scientific American* dated July 8, 1899, there were many rumors regarding the *Shamrock*. There was no speculation more improbable than the statement that the English boat was to carry a centerboard. The fate of the centerboard, as far as big yachts were concerned, was determined in 1893, when the keelboat *Valkyrie II* easily vanquished the centerboard *Vigilant* in a fifteen-mile rush to windward, against a stiff breeze. The *Valkyrie II* was the first of the ninety-footers to be built upon the fin-keel principle, just as the *Vigilant* was the last of the ninety-footers to carry a centerboard.

In 1895 the Herreshoffs abandoned the centerboard in favor of the fixed keel, the *Defender* was the first keel singlestick yacht built for the defense of the Cup. Therefore, it was not likely that Fife would return to a form of construction, which was abandoned by the people who so long used it and so thoroughly understood its possibilities.

On the subject of keels and centerboards, it is satisfactory to know that the *Columbia*, in the few trials which she had with the *Defender*, had shown, even before she had time to be "tuned up," that she was a somewhat faster boat. The difference was not remarkable, but it was obvious. Those who may have felt disappointed that she had not shown a more marked superiority must surely had remembered that it was more difficult to make a gain of five minutes over a thirty-mile course in the present era [1899] of yacht designing than it was to make one of fifteen or twenty minutes a dozen years earlier. In competitive trials between the new and old Cup defenders, we must remember that *Defender* was a phenomenally fast boat. Now, *Columbia* will probably have about five minutes advantage over *Defender* on a thirty-mile course; therefore, from twenty to twenty-five minutes better than Fife's previous ninety-foot yacht.

The *Shamrock*, the sixth British cutter seeking to capture the America's Cup was making her way across the Atlantic when the weekly *Scientific American* newspaper dated August 12. 1899, wrote of the interest to compare this new challenger's sailing qualities against previous British yachts that made the same quest:

> It is a right royal line with which this Anglo-Scotch-Irish craft is associated in holding her title of challenger; and with her Irish name, scotch design, and English construction, she is truly representative of the people to whose fostering care the early growth of the sport of yacht sailing and its present popularity are largely due.

In the dimensions and construction of both defender and challenger, there was great similarity. The *Columbia*, though stronger than the *Defender*, was a remarkably light craft, and in the *Shamrock*, Thorneycroft with his quarter of a century experience building torpedo boats, produced a hull and spars that were probably an advance over Herreshoff's boat in the matter of light scantling up-to-the-limit construction. *Shamrock's* builders kept the boat's underwater shape shrouded in secrecy, no doubt endeavoring to conceal her excessive draught; wise observers suggested it not likely that she would draw as much as 22 feet. This would mean lower lead, less of it, and a nearer approach to the true fin keel than had been shown in any 90-foot yacht since the construction of the *Pilgrim* in 1893.

A study of the two vessels reveals notable differences in their sail plans. *Shamrock's* mast appears to be stepped about two feet further aft than *Columbia's*, and her bowsprit is considerably longer, the distance from mast to outer end of bowsprit being from five to seven feet grater in *Shamrock*. Her present boom is about the same length as *Columbia's*. The gaff, topmast, and hoist of mainsail, on the other hand, are a few feet less than *Columbia's*, so that the sail plan is longer on the base line but not as lofty as that of the American boat. She probably carries a larger spinnaker, larger headsails, and a similar mainsail, the effect of which, other things being equal, should be to give *Columbia* the advantage in windward work and *Shamrock* in reaching and running. Her owner, Sir Thomas Lipton, and her designer, "Willie" Fife, have both stated that she is to carry a larger mainsail in the races on this side.

The first race took place on October 3, in the presence of the largest spectator fleet yet assembled. Neither Lipton nor Morgan sailed aboard their racing yachts; rather, they enjoyed the spectacle from their palatial steam yachts.

At the launching of Lipton's first yacht, Lady Russell christened her *Shamrock*. There was no doubt of the interest and excitement at her coming out, though every attempt to belittle her was made by the disgruntled Dunraven camp. Lipton said:

> We have engaged to win back the America's Cup. We have fairly extended ourselves, and if we are beaten, all I can say is, honor to the yacht which is better than the *Shamrock*.

The *Shamrock's* designer, William Fife Jr., said:

> Brains and all that careful thought and knowledge of naval architecture can put into a yacht are there. Every man of us is satisfied that with a fair field we shall give a tight race to any opponent.

High hopes reign at such a time. The *Shamrock* had all the points of a strong competitor, so there was reason to look forward to a close series of contests for the Cup this year.

Again, an appeal, this time by Commodore J. Pierpoint Morgan, reached Nat Herreshoff for a defender, and the answer was the bronze sloop *Columbia*, considered by many the fastest single-masted vessel ever built. Fife's *Shamrock* was easily defeated in the first and third races; she withdrew from the second after losing her topmast.

Undaunted by his loss, Lipton returned for another try at taking the Cup, with this new George Lennox Watson designed *Shamrock II*.

This period photograph postcard records the trials between the 1899 *Shamrock* and the 1901 *Shamrock II* (right) in the Ettrick Bay located on the west coast of Bute, Argyll & The Isles, Scotland.

SHAMROCK II

The weekly journal *Scientific American*, dated May 25, 1901, relates some of the characteristics of the *Shamrock II*. The paper's reporter wrote that particular interest was attached to the trial outings of the new Cup racer, insofar as her designer George Lennox Watson, applied modern scientific principles to her creation. The new boat's dimensions were very compatible with those of the *Columbia*.

By all the calculations it appeared likely that the new craft would be excessively tender, and the fact that the scanty rail with which she is provided is put eighteen inches inside the point at which the deck and topsides meet, suggests that the designer himself expected that she would heel far and easily in anything of a breeze. The fine-drawn quarters were opposed only on the ground that the want of beam there robbed the yacht of much of her power to carry sail, and this danger of having a boat which might prove unable to stand up to her work in moderate breeze was intensified by the shallower draught, less beam, steeper floor and greater height of sail plan given to *Shamrock II*, as compared with previous challengers.

In subsequent trials between the 1899 *Shamrock* and the 1901 *Shamrock II*, it was reported the current challenger was beaten by her predecessor in a strong breeze and rough sea by more than five minutes, the older boat showing superiority on every point of sailing.

These calculations looked sound, but they are contradicted in practice, for a careful observation extending through the whole of the first two days' trials shows the new challenger to be able to stand up to a breeze better than *Shamrock* and that she inclines to stiffness rather than to tenderness.

It is offered in explanation that the sails of *Shamrock II* were ill-fitting particularly the mainsail, and that she was not in proper trim. Although this is probably true, it cannot be denied that the race has been somewhat of a disappointment in England, and in America, where the interest is always greatly heightened if the challenger is believed to be a dangerous boat. The last race was over a 30-mile course the difference would have been about 8 minutes. *Columbia* beat [the first] *Shamrock* in a very similar wind and sea by 6 minutes and 31 seconds, and *Constitution* will probably be 4 or 5 minutes better than *Columbia*. This shows the challenger to be many minutes slower than she should be, if the Cup is to be carried back to the Solent.

Returning to L. Francis Herreshoff's take on the 1901-Cup race, we learn Herreshoff commends Watson's design of the *Shamrock II*; he says because the Irish boat was slightly larger than the *Columbia* and carried about 800 square feet more canvas she had to allow a forty-three second handicap to the defender.

The first race on September 28 was a 30-mile windward-leeward course in which the challenger held a very slight lead most of the time to windward and rounded the weather mark with a forty-one second lead. Spectators familiar with smaller skimming dish yachts expected the *Shamrock II* to run away from *Columbia* in the run to leeward, but the narrower *Columbia* with comparatively sharp bow surprised many when she overtook and passed the *Shamrock II* just before crossing the finish line thirty-five seconds ahead.

The second race which was started on October 1, was called off for lack of wind and it appeared the race could not be completed within the allotted time. However, *Shamrock II* did show her power by rounding the first weather mark first.

The second try to run the second race got off on October 3. A much stronger wind from the northwest of ten to twelve knots with stronger puffs later proved to be perfect for the bout. L. Francis Herreshoff praises Barr's tactical skill:

It was a triangular course and I guess Charlie Barr thought he had rather poor chances under these conditions if he were interfered with by what was supposed to be the fastest yacht on a reach, so, after luffing *Shamrock II* over the line before time, so that she would have to recross the mark and lose time, he waited until nearly the time of the second gun and started with good way on so that under these conditions he had a chance to win with *Columbia's* handicap without actually catching up with *Shamrock II*.

The third and final race of the match got off at 11:00 a.m. on October 4, for a leeward and windward course. Both yachts not wanting to be

The 1903 William Fife designed Cup challenger the *Shamrock III*.

blanked by the other in the downwind start, hung back. At the two minute warning both went over the line at practically the same time.

L. Francis Herreshoff writes that the wind at the start was from the north-west at about ten knots. He says when the yachts tacked to the west, the wind coming off the Jersey shore was more westerly and with a little more velocity, in that situation both yachts, one after the other, took the lead, and then lost the lead. "Captain Barr, with his iron nerves, sailed *Columbia* best in the last few miles of the race."

The 'old' *Columbia* beat the brand new *Shamrock II* in spite of the latter's more modern and scientific design by George Lennox Watson. The talent of Skipper Charlie Barr made the difference, because the performance of the Sir Thomas' green-colored boat was nevertheless excellent.

For spectators, this was the most exciting race of the series. The yachts swapped the lead and lost it several times, but in the run to leeward, the *Shamrock II* proved to be the fastest boat and in the last part of the run established a major lead.

SHAMROCK III

In the 1903 match, another Herreshoff creation, the 143-foot giant the *Reliance*, the largest of the Cup-defending sloops with a sail area of over 16,000 square feet, soundly defeated the third *Shamrock*.

The measurements alone of the third Lipton challenger would stand out as distinct from any of the several yachts that have crossed the Atlantic to do battle for the celebrated Cup. Until now, the challengers, with the possible exception of the *Valkyrie III*, designed by George L. Watson, have followed a distinct line of development, tracing the progress from one to the other and the efforts made in each succeeding boat to make good the apparent weaknesses of her predecessors. In the bold bid the *Shamrock II* made for success in her contest with the *Columbia* William Fife had in his designing of the *Shamrock III* strong temptation to follow the same lines. However, inspection of the new boat before the hour planned for her launch showed that Fife had chosen to return some very essential features to the type of model of the *Britannia*, whose successful defeat of the *Vigilant* led to the embodiment by Herreshoff of *Britannia*'s lines, greatly refined in the *Defender*.

It has long been a conviction among designers that the time allowance given for lack of waterline length does not put the shorter boat on a level with the yacht of greater length, and their desire has therefore been to build as near the allowable limit of 90 feet as possible. The *Shamrock III* was within a few inches of the limit, but in the matter of overall length, which goes untaxed, the new challenger was more than any Cup yacht yet built. Forward, her overhang measured 25 feet, and a similar length in the bow brought her total length from stem to stern to 140 feet.

When the underbody of the *Shamrock III* was revealed in dry dock at the Erie Basin, it corresponded very closely with the description furnished by an American spy assigned by the weekly journal *Scientific American* to view the launching.

In one paragraph, the anonymous author of an April 25, 1903 *Scientific American* article sums up the expectations of many concerning the American defender soon to face the British challenger:

> The events of the yachting seasons of 1901 and 1902, and the performance
> of certain very successful racing craft in those two years, notably the Cup

yacht *Independence*, and the sister boats *Neola* and *Weetamoe*, which more than saved their time on the Herreshoff 70-footers last year, rendered it pretty certain in the judgment of the yachting "sharpies" that, when the folding doors of the Herreshoff building shed were opened, there would pass out through them a vessel of very exaggerated proportions of the forward and after overhang of the new boat, as shown they are the work of such cautious and conservative builders as the Bristol firm.

We learn the following from the *Scientific American* dated June 27, 1903:

Shamrock III is a marked departure, in some respects, from any challenger that has been sent over from the other side for many years past. We have to go back to *Valkyrie II* to find a midship section that bears any similarity to the easy bilges and full garboards that distinguish *Shamrock III* so sharply from any of her immediate predecessors, and in this respect, she is the most "wholesome" yacht of any of the existing challengers and defenders of the 90-foot class. Having said this much, it has to be admitted that all the other characteristic features of the boat are marked by the extremes of beam, draft, and overall length to which designers have been driven in their attempt to carry a maximum amount of sail under a rule which, unfortunately, puts no limit whatever upon sail area—an unfortunate omission, to which more than anything else is to be attributed the absurdly exaggerated proportions of the modern racing 90-footer. Although her midship section is large, the lines, which have been carried out with the skill that characterizes all the Fife boats, are so sweet and fair that she looks at first glance more like a 70-footer than a boat built up to the full 90-foot limit.

All period reports indicate that with her exaggerated proportions, the *Reliance* had a strong family likeness to earlier Herreshoff boats. In drawing out her lines to such an extreme length, Herreshoff produced an extremely handsome craft. The hard turn of the midship sections at the bilges is softened out gradually as the forward and after ends of the waterline are reached, with the result that the overhangs themselves are very symmetrical and show a sweetness of modeling that goes far to redeem their disproportional length. The deck line does not flow toward the bow and stern with so flat a curve as had been customary in earlier

Herreshoff boats, with the result that when she heels, she will take a very long bearing, and there will be no hard spot or shoulder to pile up the water when driven at high speed.

One of the most striking features in the boat is the long, drawn-out bow projecting nearly thirty feet beyond the waterline. The *Scientific American* writer echoed the concerns of many seasoned yachtsmen who wondered why the bow was not made shorter relative to the stern, reasoning that every foot of length can be utilized. No greater authority than Herreshoff regarded the *Reliance* as something of an experiment; he said that only the actual test in a jump of sea off Newport or Sandy Hook could determine the value of such an extreme bow.

The following is an excerpt from Nat Herreshoff's 1934 recollection of the *Reliance*:[7]

In the fall of 1902, there was another challenge for the America's Cup and the order was given us about [the] first of November. We had already taken [an] order for an eighty-six feet waterline schooner [*Ingomar*], and the class of Bar Harbor thirty-One Footers (11), and others besides the usual number of steamers. So, our shops were quite full. Mr. Iselin had recovered his health and again became manager of a new Cup defender, this the fourth time. A syndicate of very distinguished yachtsmen of the New York Yacht Club owned her. She became to be named *Reliance* and to carry out Mr. Iselin's wishes, she favored too much of the scow type, above the water, to be a good type of big yacht. She was very powerful, having about one hundred eight and one-half tons of lead low down. She was one hundred and forty-three feet overall, ninety feet waterline, twenty-five feet nine inches beam, with bronze plating over a steel frame of my longitudinal plan of construction, and very strong for its weight, though hardly equal to the pounding due to [the] scow form of bow. Her rig was enormous [with a] boom [of] one hundred and fifteen feet four inches by twenty-four inches diameter, [a] gaff [of] seventy-two feet, [a] #1 club topsail yard [of] sixty-eight feet, [a] spinnaker boom [of] eighty-three feet four inches and others in proportion. The #1 club topsail reached one hundred eighty-nine feet six inches above water and bowsprit end to boom end was two hundred and two feet eight inches. All the major spars were steel. Her mainsails were probably the largest ever made and were of 000 and 0000 duck. He [Mr. Islin] made four, I think, all of specially woven duck for the purpose. Her crew was sixty-eight all told, and Charles Barr was captain. With the exception of the main boom being lengthened two and one-half feet and [the] gaff two feet, so she would balance well with [a] larger sized jib topsail, there was no change made on her and she never had any accidents to require new parts or changes except reinforcing the plating under the bow two or three times. Both *Constitution* and *Columbia* were fitted out for trial craft and [with the *Reliance*] they made a noble trio.

[The] *Reliance* proved always faster to windward and before the wind, but not any faster in reaching, and in fact, not as fast as [the] *Constitution*. This could not be explained, for due to a much longer bilge line and longer useful length due to extreme overhangs, it was expected this would be her best point of sailing. These trials demonstrated *Constitution* to be faster than *Columbia* as was indicated in their early meetings.

I sailed in most of *Reliance's* races and often took the helm, so [Charles] Barr could check up the trim of sails or rest. She easily defended the Cup against *Shamrock III*. It is interesting that in the first unfinished race, started in a light north westerly and quite a ground swell, in going fifteen miles to leeward with spinnakers and pounding into the seas, we ran away from *Shamrock* between two and three miles. [The] race was called off in calm.

The *Reliance* and the *Shamrock III* eventually met in late August; the *Reliance* won the first meet by seven minutes, due largely to bad sail handling by the British boat's crew. The *Reliance* won the second race by one minute, nineteen seconds, corrected time. Then, because of a lack of wind, the third race was delayed for nine days, with a one-day delay for fear of the yachts being demasted because of near-gale-force winds.

The 1903 series finished on September 3 in foggy weather. The race came to its awkward finish when *Shamrock III* became lost in the fog, totally missing the mark and winding up northeast of the lightship.

SHAMROCK IV

Lipton challenged again in 1914 under the new rating rule. However, World War I interrupted plans to build yachts for the challenge and defense, so the Cup was safe in the halls of the New York Yacht Club for the duration.

Lipton's *Shamrock IV* won the first two of the scheduled five races, the closest of all his attempts to capture the coveted Cup.

Plans came together in 1920 for the long anticipated match, and the Cup was up for grabs once again. Lipton brought out *Shamrock IV* to meet another Herreshoff creation, the *Resolute*.

Charles Nicholson, *Shamrock's* designer, included a fatal error in his design when it called for a water line of 4 feet (110 feet 4 inches) greater than *Resolute* (106 feet 4 inches), which meant she had to carry more sail than the *Resolute* and therefore allowing her adversary as much as seven minutes and fifteen seconds handicap.

In the opening match on July 15, the *Resolute* was forced to resign the race after an error in sail handling; her mainsail halyard broke, thereby allowing *Shamrock IV* the win. The second race took place on July 20, and Lipton's yacht won it by 2 minutes and 26 seconds corrected time.

Faced with the third and possibly the final race, and loss of the Cup, Capt. Nat was whisked overnight, aboard a US Navy destroyer, to adjust the *Resolute's* rig. Capt. Nat intimately knew his design and tweaked her to be the unbridled champion he had created.

The J-class *Shamrock V* was Lipton's fifth and mightiest sailor commissioned but she was no match against Vanderbilt's *Enterprise*.

In race three, on the windward-leeward course, following a demanding nineteen tacks, the *Resolute* held the lead. However, the *Shamrock IV*, a powerful racer skippered by professional Captain William Burton, fought back and the racers crossed the finish line in a dead heat. The Committee gave the win to the *Resolute* on a corrected time of 7 minutes and 1 second. The margins of *Resolute's* victories increased in the next two races in which she proved herself the faster boat with a crew who worked with military-like correctness. The *Resolute* successfully defended the Cup with a 3-2 victory on July 27 with a corrected time win of 19 minutes and 45 seconds.

THE *SHAMROCK V*

The *Shamrock V* was Sir Tom's fifth and final attempt to capture the America's Cup. She was designed by Charles Nicholson and built in the

Camper & Nicholson yard in Gasport, Hampshire, England; she was the first British yacht built to the J-Class Rule. *Shamrock V* was sturdily built: mahogany planking over steel frames, yellow pine deck, and teak used for stem and stern posts and counter-timbers, hollow spruce mast; she had lower sail area but greater rig height relative to other 1930 Js. She was extensively tuned in England before the races. Her vital statistics are no less impressive: her waterline length was 81 feet 1 inch, overall length 119 feet 8 inches, she displaced 134 tons, and her sail area was slightly less than *Enterprise* at 7,540 square feet.

The yacht continued being modified after launch—her hull shape and rudder were changed, as was also her rig to create the most effective racing sail plan.

Geoffrey F. Hammond in his *Showdown at Newport* writes:

> The Cup match itself was a rout, the worst defeat suffered by any of Sir Thomas Lipton's five challengers. Aboard his power yacht *Erin*; the 82-year old Lipton watched what he knew was his last chance dissolving before his tired eyes.

CHAPTER NINE

1899: *Shamrock vs. Columbia*

Having delighted the Princess of Wales with a very generous and public gift, Lipton then turned to help her husband, the prince. Owner of the world's most recognized yacht—*Britannia*—and commodore of the Royal Yacht Squadron, Edward, Prince of Wales, was to a degree, personally responsible for the future of America's Cup challenges. As the third anniversary of Dunraven's ignoble retreat approached, none of the usual millionaire yachtsmen came forward to make a challenge on behalf of Great Britain. Lipton meanwhile, allowed his name to be floated as a potential sponsor.

——Michael D'Antonio, *A Full Cup*, 2010

COMPARING *COLUMBIA* AND *SHAMROCK*

An abridged and edited article published in *Scientific American*, August 12, 1899 by an anonymous writer.

The *Shamrock's* mast appears to be stepped about 2 feet further aft than the *Columbia's* and her bowsprit is considerably longer, the distance from mast to the outer end of the bowsprit is 5 to 7 feet greater in the *Shamrock*. Her present boom is about the same length as the *Columbia's*. The gaff, topmast, and hoist of mainsail, are a few feet less than *Columbia*, so that the sail plan is longer on the base line, however not as lofty as that of Nat Herreshoff's boat. She probably carries a larger spinnaker, larger headsails, and a smaller mainsail, the effect of which, other things being equal, should be to give the *Columbia* the advantage in windward work and the *Shamrock* in reaching and running. Her owner, Lipton and her designer, Fife have both stated that she is to carry a larger mainsail in the races in American waters.

A fairly reliable comparison of the sailing qualities of the two boats is obtained by studying the remarkable series of races sailed by the *Britannia* and *Vigilant* in 1894, and comparing the results with the performance in North American waters of the *Vigilant* against *Defender* in 1895, and the *Defender* against *Columbia* in 1899, and with recent trials in England of the *Britannia* against *Shamrock*.

Of course, the value of such comparisons depends upon the boats the *Vigilant* and *Britannia* being as fast in subsequent years as they were in 1894. There is no doubt that they were in as good condition, and possibly better. The *Vigilant* was improved in 1895, by removal of 43,000 pounds of lead from the inside and the addition of 53,000 pounds to the outside of the keel. The *Britannia*, in addition to the improvement in trim, and sail plan, due to three years of continuous racing, her hull was re-coppered, her topsides replaced and carefully smoothed off, and her wood boom was replaced by one of steel, before she raced the *Shamrock*.

The *Vigilant* and the *Britannia* competed in seventeen races, of which the *Britannia* won eleven. This appears to indicate a decided advantage of the *Britannia* in winds of certain strength. In races sailed at an average speed of eight knots or less, the *Britannia* usually won, and her wins were larger the lighter the wind. However, when the wind averaged a speed exceeding eight knots, it was the *Vigilant's* day, and the harder the blow, the greater her margin of victory.

Well known nineteenth-century British yachting authority Dixon Kemp, when summing up the season's races, pronounced the boats about equal.

When the *Shamrock* and the *Columbia* have settled their little affair next week, the race will have been the tenth since the proud day when the eagle first acquired a right to perch upon that trophy.

      ——Anonymous Boston newspaper sport writer's comment,

                September 24, 1899.

A discussion of the details of racing models as they have evolved since the last round of Cup races is too technical to relate here.[8] Without attempting

n this 1895 Judge Magazine's satirical cartoon, Lord Dunraven is pictured as a cry-baby after his *Valkyrie III's* embarrassing
eat by Herreshoff's *Defender*.

HARPER'S WEEKLY.

A

JOURNAL OF CIVILIZATION.

Vol. XXXI.—No. 1606.
Copyright, 1887, by Harper & Brothers.

NEW YORK, SATURDAY, OCTOBER 1, 1887.

TEN CENTS A COPY.
WITH A SUPPLEMENT.

JONATHAN AND SANDY.

2. The Harper's Weekly illustrated newspaper published this satirical cartoon showing Uncle Sam teasing the kilt-wearing Scot in the paper's October 1, 1887 edition. Scotland sent over the *Thistle*, which was soundly scuttled by the *Volunteer* in two matches.

VOL. XXXVIII. No. 965.

PUCK BUILDING, New York, September 4th, 1895.
Copyright, 1895, by Keppler & Schwarzmann.

PRICE 10 CENTS.

Puck

Entered at N. Y. P. O. as Second-class Mail Matter.

THAT COVETED CUP.

UNCLE SAM.—Wa-al, old feller, you 've got another chance to look at it, anyhow, even if you can't win it!

3. In this September 4, 1895 PUCK cartoon satirizes a portly John Bull admiring the America's Cup, while Uncle Sam says, "You've got another chance to look at it, anyway, even if you can't win it."

VOL. L. No. 1282.

PUCK BUILDING, New York, September 25th, 1901.
Copyright, 1901, by Keppler & Schwarzmann.

PRICE TEN

"What fools these Mortals be!"

Puck

Entered at N. Y. P. O. as Second-class M

A SPECIALIST'S OPINION.

WELL GUARDED.

5. In this August 3, 1903 PUCK cartoon, Sir Tom is pictured "Romancing the Cup."

6. The satirical PUCK cartoon pictures a nautically attired bulldog keeping guard over the Cup.

4. The New York satirical weekly, the PUCK dated September 16, 1901 lampoons Lawson's and Herreshoff's sadness at the New York Yacht Club's rejection of their Cup defender candidates, the *Independence* and the *Constitution*.

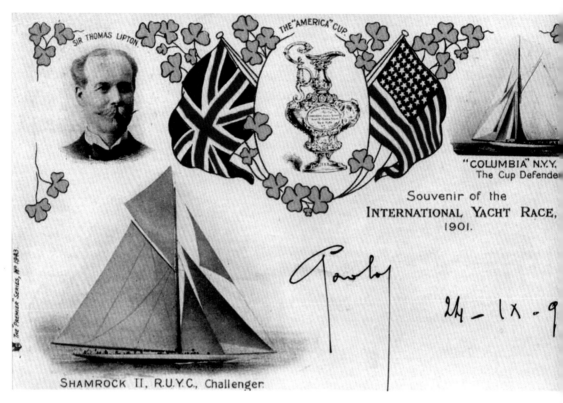

7. Romantic images of the challenger, defender and Sir Tom on this souvenir postcard of the "1901 International Yacht Race."

8. A lithograph tin souvenir pin back.

9. The humorous carton from Harper's Weekly, dated October 1, 1887 pictures Uncle Sam aboard the *Columbia* taunting Sir Tom aboard his *Shamrock II* with the coveted Cup.

Over a period of thirty-years, spending hundreds of thousands of dollars, Lipton built five magnificent racing yachts but he could not retrieve the prestigious America's Cup to celebrate the glory of the United Kingdom's yachting pride.

The following eleven color images are watercolor illustrations by artist W.S. Tomkin that Lipton commissioned for use on Christmas cards he sent to friendly American yachtsmen and other admirers. The author had the good fortune to acquire several of these very scarce Christmas cards and is pleased to share them with readers.

Sir Tom's Christmas greeting reads: "With my kindest thoughts for Christmas and the best of Good Wishes for the New Year." Signed: *Thomas J. Lipton.*

10. The cover of Lipton's 1920 Christmas card.

11. The *Shamrock IV* (the green boat) nearly overtakes the *Resolute* at sandy Hook on July 21, 1902.

12. Lipton's 1922 Christmas greeting is an illustration of his Dambatenne bungalow, Haputale; his home when in sunny Ceylon.

SHAMROCK LEAVING CITY ISLAND, NEW YORK

GREETINGS 1923

13. The cover of Lipton's 1923 Christmas card illustrates the Shamrock leaving City Island, New York.

14. Artist W.S. Tomkin's dramatic conception of the *Shamrock* homeward bound in ocean-going rig, weathering a mid-Atlantic storm, September, 1923.

15. The *Shamrock* racing in the Solent against the *Britannia* (left) and the *White Heather* for the International Gold Challenge Cup, August 9, 1924: race won by the *Shamrock*.

16. Sir Tom's 1925 Christmas card cover.

17. The start of the last race of the 1925 season at Dartmouth. Left to right the yachts are: *White Heather* and the *Lulworth* (neck to neck); the *Westward*, the *Britannia*, and the *Shamrock* in the lead; the race won by the *Shamrock*.

18. In this 1926 Christmas card, artist W.S. Tomkin paints this delightful representation of Lipton's bungalow and garden near Kandy in Ceylon.

19. The *Shamrock* racing with the *Britannia, Lulworth,* and *White Heather* at Cowes, 1927.

20. The sloop America with its winning of the great international yacht race at Cowes, England in 1851 started the quest for the Cup by yacht clubs worldwide with access to the sea. Published in 1903 by the Detroit Photographic Co.

21. In the 1886 race, the *Mayflower* designed by William Burges for the New York Yacht Club beat England's *Galaten*, 2-0. Published in 1903 by the Detroit Photographic Co.

22. Nat Herreshoff creates a truly great flyer in the *Vigilant* and wins 3-0 against the *Valkyrie II* in 1893. Published in 1903 by the Detroit Photographic Co.

23. Pictured is Lipton's *Shamrock II*, which lost to Herreshoff's *Columbia* 3-0 in the 1901 races. Lithograph is No.1881 in the Wrench series, published in Saxony.

24. In the 1901 Cup races, the *Shamrock II* (foreground) and the *Columbia* battled it out, the *Columbia* winning 3-0. Published in 1903 by the Detroit Photographic Co.

25. Herreshoff's magnificent Cup Defender the *Reliance* set 16,000 square feet of sail to triumph over Lipton's *Shamrock III* in the 1903 matchup. Published in 1903 by the Detroit Photographic Co.

26. The *Shamrock III* was a beautiful craft, but it could not defeat the *Reliance*. The America's Cup races are not a beauty contest. Published in 1903 by the Detroit Photographic Co.

27. Lipton came back in 1930 with his J-class entry, the *Shamrock V*; he was vanquished by Harold Vanderbilt's *Enterprise*, in Rhode Island Sound by 4-0. Post card published by R.S. Art Press Ltd., England.

to gain strict accuracy at the risk of being unintelligible, it may be said that the Yankee notion at the start was a rather beamy vessel, with a center-board to make her hold on to the wind, while the British thought on the matter was in a deep boat for power, with sharp lines for speed.

Among the most pronounced changes in both challenger and defender is the length of the keel. Previously, when the elements of a yacht's makeup controlled designers because of their rudimentary knowledge on questions of wetted surface, shape of the lateral plane, and other such matters, the fore and aft under bodies were not cut as they are in contemporary models. This can be seen in the jump American yachts made from the 1893 *Vigilant*, with a keel length of 48 feet and the *Defender*[9] of 1895, with 35 feet, and from the later to fewer than 29 feet on the most recent production, the *Columbia* of the Herreshoff Manufacturing Company.

Another matter of interest is while the *Columbia* is so nearly like the *Defender* only the most expert eye could find the points of improvement in the former when the two were side by side. The *Shamrock* and the *Columbia* were so similar that one London yachting journal wrote as much before at the time of *Shamrock's* launch.

With the first sign of motion came lusty cheers from 5000 throats, ear-piercing shrieks from strident whistles, and salutes from yacht cannon. The scene was spectacular. It was rendered more theatric still because of the powerful calcium lights flashed on the shapely hull from the tender *St Michael*.

As the *Columbia* emerged from the [construction] shed Captain Charles Barr along with designer-builder Nat Herreshoff and a half dozen sailors, was on her deck, erected a flagstaff and broke out an immense silken yacht ensign. A few moments later, the private signals of her owners, Commodore Morgan and Mr. Iselin, were displayed from a jury-mast stepped in the aperture for the immense spar of Oregon pine, which is to be placed in position immediately. The darkness of the night was made brilliant by the flashlights of the photographers and the glare of searchlights, all aimed at the hull of white and gold moving with grace and dignity to its baptism of seawater. Seventeen minutes elapsed before the stately craft floated clear of the cradle and danced buoyantly in the element she is destined to adorn.

The secrecy, which surrounds the construction of the competing yachts, always awakens more than usual curiosity as to the form and construction of the boats. It is believed that the extraordinary precautions, which are taken, prevent the opposing syndicate's spies from getting even a hint as the challenger or defender's beam, draught, or lines of the craft. It is for this reason the *Columbia* was launched at night and the *Shamrock*'s shape shroud-covered.

The dry-docking of the yachts has furnished a great surprise; for where the public was expecting novelties it found the case of both challenger and defender nothing more or less than a typical, up-to-date yacht. The characteristics of the type, as represented in a ninety-footer are a beam of about twenty four feet and a draught of twenty feet; some eighty to ninety tons of lead on the keel; a displacement of from one hundred forty to one hundred fifty tons; and a sail area of about thirteen thousand square feet. The construction materials include nickel steel for the framing, with plating of non-corrosive bronze and hollow steel spars of great strength and lightness.

——Scientific American, October 14, 1899.

Taking the *Columbia* and the *Shamrock* as examples, the average viewer with some knowledge of sailing vessels will agree that they conform with amazing closeness to the specifications listed above—as far as dimensions and materials are concerned. In the matter of model, both above and below the water line, there are, very marked differences between the two boats: but in no sense did either hold any surprises. The Herreshoff model possesses all the characteristics, which distinguish a Herreshoff design from a Fife design, and they certainly present no startling novelties, previously unknown or untried by yacht designers. The *Columbia* was an improved *Defender*, and the *Shamrock* an enlarged and improved *Isolde*.

Compared with the *Defender* of 1895, the *Columbia* was in every way a more handsome yacht. In the dry dock photos (seen elsewhere in this volume) what delicate beauty the skillful designer imparts to the underwater form even to a deep fin keel vessel of this extreme type. The variations from the *Defender* are all in the track of securing an improved form, one that can be driven through the water with less expenditure of power. While the beam is wider and the lead placed lower, the overhang and waterline length are considerably larger and finer than the older boat. The hull is deeper, and the whole model is a further departure even than was that of the *Defender* from the old skimming dish type of hull, the construction, moreover, is sturdier than that of the *Defender* because the perfidious aluminum alloy in the ribs, deck beams, and topside with more reliable steel and bronze.

EVALUATING THE COMPETITORS

The *Shamrock*, Lipton's first yacht, as far as construction is concerned, she was very much like Herreshoff's *Defender*. She was the largest challenger ever to enter the fray. Built flat and broad, she measured almost 90 feet at waterline, carrying 13,492 square feet of sail.

In the *Shamrock*, the British sent over their first ever-racing machine. She is the lightest of her size ever constructed, even with the exception of the *Defender*; reports surfaced saying that in her aluminum deck alone there was a saving of 5,000 pounds. Perhaps the most striking features of the boat are her unusually lofty topsides—her freeboard is over five feet as against three and a half feet in the *Columbia*—and her deep draught of twenty-one and a half feet.

Her midship section shows a considerable flare above the waterline, and this, combined with her wide beam, high freeboard, and deep lead, gives her great sail-carrying power, especially in a strong wind. The boat has rather a hand bilge and a flat floor, which rounds into the fin proper with a short hard curve. When afloat she looks to be much bigger than she is, most of the boat being above the waterline, and as a glance at the midship sections of the two vessels will show, she approaches more nearly to the true fin keel type than does the *Columbia*. The sheer plan shows that the *Shamrock's* keel is much the longer—about eight or nine feet longer—hence the center of gravity of the lead is lower, and this coupled with the fact that her draught is deeper by one and a half feet makes it certain that the center of gravity of the lead is at least three feet deeper below the waterline in the English boat. Other things being equal, this means less lead for the same stability. At the same time the longer keel involves the addition slower boat in light winds. In heavy winds, and indeed in any wind, the longer keel should make the *Shamrock* a better boat in climbing to windward when close-hauled.

The October 14, 1899 edition of the weekly Scientific American journal of science published this full-page illustration of the *Columbia* at the Brooklyn Navy Yard and the *Shamrock* at the Brooklyn Erie Basin, photographs which expose the Cup challenger's and defender's underwater configurations formally shrouded in secrecy.

Earlier challengers sailed across the Atlantic to the site of the race for the Cup. The *Shamrock*, however, was towed most of the way across behind Lipton's palatial steam yacht the *Erin*.

The problems faced by all designers of sea-going racing sail-craft are the increase of the sail carrying power and the decrease of the resistance of the hull in passing through the water. Sail carrying power is obtained by giving the yacht plenty of beam, and further increasing it by giving her depth and placing the ballast at the lowest point of the keel. Resistance to the water is diminished by making that part of the vessel, which is under water as small as possible. To accomplish this, the designer cuts away the forward part of the underbody of their vessels so that the whole bow is nothing but a long, narrow blade. Then the bilge is raised—the shoulder formed at the point where the inward and downward curve of the side begins—as high as possible. A deep keel, with some ninety tons of lead at its extreme lower edge, completes the outfit.

Both the *Columbia* and the *Shamrock* show all these features. The only true difference between the two yachts is in the proportion of length to breadth. This is the result of the use of slightly conflicting theories Nat Herreshoff and William Fife, the two designers. The difference is so small that to any eye but that of a true expert it means nothing at all.

The greatest care was taken by the *Shamrock's* designer to keep her dimensions secret but an authoritative London daily news journal released some of the secrets in an article that gave away some of the most salient details of the boats dimensions. The figures are as follow: length over all, 132 feet 2 inches; water line length, 89 feet 6 inches; beam, 24 feet 6 inches; and draft, 20 feet. Her sail area 14,125 square feet and her displacement at 147 tons.

The *Columbia's* dimensions were kept equally secret, but they were discovered by some subterfuge and reported in the same journal. She is 131 feet over all; 89-feet 6 inches water line length; 24 feet 2 inches beam; and 19 feet 10 inches draft. Her reported sail area was 13,940 square feet.

W. J. Henderson the sport editor for *Munsey's Magazine* (August 1899) writes:

> If the figures of the English newspapers are correct, the challenger may have
> to allow the defender a small handicap. This is less of an advantage to the

recipient than is the usual case. It is an advantage in very light weather, but when there is a good breeze a big boat always bests the smaller one. The fourteen inches greater length and four inches greater beam of the *Shamrock* should make her a slightly more powerful vessel than the *Columbia* in either light or heavy weather; but there may be something in the shape of her hull to overcome the benefit of the extra power. There can hardly be any room for doubt that Mr. Fife has designed a very fast light weather yacht; but so has Mr. Herreshoff.

Henderson continues with his sober observation of the *Columbia's* ability to glide effortlessly through the water when there are not enough breezes to raise a ruffle on the surface of the sea:

> She also has a very pretty trick of lying over on her side and racing like a steamship when there is a good breeze and smooth water.
>
> Those who are familiar with handling small recreational "sandbaggers" will realize after reading the specifications of the two antagonists of the immense size and power of these giant sloops that will battle for the America's Cup. The *Columbia* carries a spar that towers to the height of more than one hundred forty feet above the water; her main boom is more than one hundred feet long, and the canvas in her mainsail weighs more than one ton. These same figures also apply in a general way to the *Shamrock*, so when these two giants eventually met, there was a veritable struggle of the Titans.

No essay on the subject of America's Cup yachts is complete without some discussion of the enormous cost (in 1899 dollars) of conducting these remarkable races. The following discourse concerning the cost of the event is an anonymous sport writer's report published in the August 1899 edition of *Munsey's Magazine*.

> Last, but not least, comes the element of expense in conducting there remarkable races. They are the most costly sporting contests in this up to date world, and the bills would make even Nero and Heliogabalus gasp and stare. It costs about $75,000 to build and fit out a sloop like the *Columbia*, and then the expense has just begun. The crew numbers thirty men, and to these must be added a captain, who commands high wages; a mate who is also

not a cheap man; and the cooks and stewards. Then there are the endless repairs and alterations, and the tender—in this case, a little steamer [the] *St. Michaels*, hired for the entire season to go about with the *Columbia* to tow her when necessary and to keep her spare gear on board. It is easy to see that if $150,000 were banked to the *Columbia's* credit in June, there would be no balance by the middle of October. But there is also the *Defender*. She had to be fitted out for the season, and has to be kept in commission all summer as a trial horse.

Sir Thomas Lipton's expenditures must be almost, if not quite, as large. In addition to building the *Shamrock*, he purchased the *Erin*, a large steam yacht, to accompany her across the ocean and to act as a consort to her on this side. Sir Thomas and his friends will live on the *Erin* and their account will not be paid in shillings.

The New York Yacht Club also shoulders a share of the pecuniary burden, it provides the necessary tugs for measuring and marking the courses, and has many other small incidental expenses.[10] It appears, therefore, that a struggle for the America's Cup costs, all told, about half a million of dollars. Such an outlay on the single sporting contest demonstrates the shallowness of the old saying that horseracing is the sport of kings. Only the financial monarchs of our modern period could dream of entering upon the pursuit of such a formidably costly game as yacht racing for the championship of the world.

During the season the *Columbia* raced many other sloops and particularly against the *Defender*. At the time, the practice was to have a trial race for the honor of being the official Cup defender of record. Early in September, the *Columbia* defeated the *Defender* twice, thus securing the defender's honor.

RACE ONE

After all is said and done, when the starting gun is fired and the timekeeper records the expired racing time, should the *Shamrock* prevail, preparations to bring the Cup back were already being discussed.

If the *Columbia* wins, as all-good Americans hope, and most of them firmly believe she will, there will come such a paean of victory from the guns and steam whistles as will rouse old father Neptune from his lair. But if the challenger should be the better yacht, than her crew will learn that Americans know how to appreciate the valor and skill of a worthy foe.

The *Shamrock* was in the capable hands of Captain Archie Hogarth, one of the most accomplished professional yacht skippers in Britain; Lipton, not of maritime bearing himself, selected Peter Donaldson, reputed to be the most crack amateur yachtsman in England as his on board representative.

The *Columbia* was in equally good hands. Her sailing master, Captain Charles Barr, a naturalized American from Scotland was recognized as one of the most perceptive sailors of large yachts. Barr selected his crew of Yankee sailors from Deer Island, Maine, a place with the reputation of producing the best sailors in America.

All summer, Barr drilled his men in their duties carried out in frequent races with the *Defender* as trial horse, so by the time of the matches his Yankee crew was familiar with every strand of line on the *Columbia*, and treaded around the craft as steadily as a family of sure-footed cats.

The racecourse was off Sandy Hook, and the contest was decided by the winning of two out of three matches. The courses were alternately fifteen miles to windward and return, and around a triangular course of ten miles on each side. These courses give abundant opportunities to test the yachts and the skippers on every point of sailing. The better vessel was bound to be victorious provided she was not the subject of bad handling.

The October 14 issue of the weekly journal *Scientific American* reported two unsuccessful attempts to sail the first race of the series. We learn the winds were too light to afford any reliable test of the yachts, for although the *Columbia* was the leading boat during the greater part of the contests, on both occasions the *Shamrock* was slightly in the lead when the race was called off. In spite of the fact, however, the challenger showed unexpected light weather qualities; judging the performance of the two yachts indicated the *Columbia* to be the better all-round weather boat under the prevailing conditions.

The initial match was scheduled for October 3 and at the time of the start, there appeared a large flotilla of excursion steamers carrying the public to the racecourse; these boats were in company of yachts owned by Sir Tom, J. P. Morgan and other wealthy individuals.

The allotted time for the race was five and one half hours, over a course of windward and leeward of fifteen miles to a leg. At the gun, there was a light northeast breeze so the yachts were given a leeward start with the course down the Jersey shore.

The *Shamrock* crossed the line almost three quarters of a minute ahead of the *Columbia* giving her enough time to have her air free. However, it was a very fluky day, and about one hour after the start, the *Columbia* managed to get a draft of fresh air which pushed her past the *Shamrock* allowing her to round the lee mark two minutes in the lead; on the way home the wind slackened so that the yachts could not finish within the allotted time.

Over the next two weeks several attempts were made to finish a race, but each attempt was aborted by an unusual spell of fog and calm.

RACE TWO

After trying daily to run the race, it was not until October 16 that a race was completed.

The race of October 16 started in a moderate east wind with light fog and chop of sea. The course was windward and leeward. The *Shamrock* got to the start by a few seconds, the sea chop seeming not to bother her. The *Columbia* with her moderately sharp bow went so well that shortly she was dead to windward of the challenger where she stayed for the rest of the leg and rounded the outer mark more than nine minutes ahead of the *Shamrock*.

On the run home, the *Columbia* gained and won the race by ten minutes eight seconds corrected time.

L. Francis Herreshoff had the following comment on the race of October 17:

> The next day the wind was still east but the fog had cleared away leaving quite a lop of a sea. This time the race was a triangle of thirty miles with the first leg to windward, there was quite a lot of jockeying at this start, and Captain Hogarth of *Shamrock* proved to be as good as Charlie Barr for they went over the starting line lapped with *Shamrock* two seconds ahead, but *Columbia*

to weather. The two yachts sailed very evenly indeed in the first part of the race and, though the wind was only moderate, about half an hour after the start *Shamrock's* top mast broke at the cap iron letting her club topsail and all its gear go to leeward. According to an agreement in these Cup races, if one of the competitors was crippled the other was to continue the race, which *Columbia* was forced to do, but not being in competition, she lowered her jib topsail in spite of which she covered the triangular course in a little fewer than ten knots.

RACE THREE

On October 19, The *Shamrock* took on about four tons of ballast and was remeasured, with the result that she now had to give the *Columbia* a time allowance. On the 20th, they took to the sea again. The weather was cold with a brisk north wind of about twenty knots; the course was a windward and leeward one with the first leg off the wind.

For this race, the committee chose to use what is called a two-gun start in which each contestant is clocked by the actual time it takes the yacht to cover the course.[11]

Therefore, the *Columbia* started about one minute after the *Shamrock*. On the run to the lee the *Columbia* had a great deal of trouble carrying her spinnaker which seemed to balloon up very high and cause her long spinnaker boom to bend alarmingly while *Shamrock's* spinnaker behaved well.

Throughout this match, the *Columbia* outpointed and out footed the *Shamrock*. All the time on the windward leg the *Columbia* had her working topsail hoisted ready to break out, but she was doing so well they did not use it. Captain Barr and the *Columbia's* designer Captain Nat Herreshoff sailed her so well on the last leg that she won with corrected time by six minutes, thirty-four seconds.

L. Francis Herreshoff remarked that in his opinion, she probably could have won by a greater margin after she was so far ahead if she had used her topsail, however, Charlie Barr and Nat Herreshoff just played safe so as not to strain her spars and other gear.

At a banquet after the race, a compassionate woman, in the party of guests, told Lipton she had heard that the Americans had "put something in the water" to prevent him from winning. To this Lipton, with tongue tucked tightly in his cheek replied, "You are correct madam, they had put the *Columbia* in the water for just that very purpose."

CHAPTER TEN

Why the Shamrock II Cannot Win

In quiet little Bristol, Rhode Island, where the Wizard and his men put finishing touches on *Columbia*, they regarded Lipton as ignorant, misinformed,
and more interested in publicity than sailing.

—Michael D'Antonio, *A Full Cup*, 2010

An article by A. J. Kenealy published in the September 21, 1901 issue of
Leslie's Weekly Magazine:

The first time I saw *Shamrock II* was when she arrived at the Erie Basin,
after her long tow across the ocean. Being an old sailor, I was naturally
impressed with the exquisite beauty of her lines. Mr. Watson is famous the
world over for the shapely hulls he has "created." In this craft, he has fairly
surpassed himself. The jury lower-mast and stump top-mast, the lack of a
bowsprit, and the disfigurement that always attends a modern racing yacht
when rigged for an ocean voyage, though detracting slightly from her good
looks, by no means obscured the symmetry of her form. I expected a reve-
lation of rare import when the whole of her hull should be shown naked to
a few privileged sightseers in the dry dock. When she first plunged into the
Clyde a pontoon partially concealed her from the gaze of the vulgar—even
as canvas petticoats draped about the first *Shamrock* protected her from
the prying eyes of reporters and the curious lenses of photographers when
launched into the Thames. Thus, no accurate presentment of the challenger
was available, and consequently all hands were agog with inquisitiveness.

It had been cabled across that Mr. Watson had profited by a series of
experiments in the big tank at Dumbarton, that he had devised something
new, striking, daringly original in the annals of naval architecture. A dark hint

or two as to a new combination of the "cod's head and mackerel's tail" —that singular delusion of our daddies—added new zest to speculations. Can it be wondered at if all of us interested in the sport expected that Mr. Watson had at last evolved an epoch-making yacht—a *Gloriana*, for instance—that would revolutionize yacht designing and make his name as famous as that of the Wizard of Bristol, R.I. For four hours I was one of a group that watched the water recede from the sides of *Shamrock II*. Inch by inch the underbody was exposed to the eager eyes glued on her. Soon it became evident that there was no new feature in her design, and that Mr. Watson when at work on her had *Columbia* in his mind as the basis of his model. He could not have done better.

Mr. Watson deserves the highest praise for producing such a good-looking craft. He might have turned out as great an eyesore as the first *Shamrock*—the least beautiful Cup challenger that ever came here—barring the Canadian sloop *Atalanta*. [The] *Shamrock II*, should set as an object lesson to some of our building naval architects who seem to have no perception of beauty, as far as their art is concerned. If this should come to pass the visit of the new *Shamrock* shall not have been in vain.

In the rig of the challenger, in my judgment, is superior to that of the American yacht. I do not like the telescoping top-mast invented by Nat Herreshoff. I do not approve of the double spreaders, which support the masts of the *Constitution*. I think a yacht should be so sparred and rigged that her mast will stay on end and not topple over the side. I believe in a bobstay and dolphin striker sufficiently stout to support the bowsprit. It may seem bold for a man like myself, brought up as a sailor, to presume to criticize a designer of such scientific attainments as Nat Herreshoff, but in my judgment he runs too many risks by sacrificing strength to lightness, I am aware that no disaster has ever happened to one of his yachts while actually defending the Cup, except when Lord Dunraven's *Valkyrie III*, ran into the *Defender*. This, I think is due to the good luck which attends Nat Herreshoff. Some people urge that the collapse of a mast in a tuning-up spin has no more significance than a woman's shedding of her hair pins in a ballroom. From a theoretical point of view, the loss of ever so many spars may not amount to much, but dismasting has a demoralizing effect on a crew and thus works disastrously. In a piping breeze it is not reassuring for Jack to be continually speculating just how soon it will be before the whole top hamper aloft comes down by the run about his ears. Or for him to have a bet pending with his shipmate as to whether the spreader will part farther out or closer in than it did on the previous occasion, the yacht sailor is human. He is, in fact, choke full of crotchets. Some not untruthfully call him a crank, as a matter of fact, he is not yet educated up to the down to-date spider's web kind of a rig that the Herreshoffs effect. He cannot realize why a steel lower-mast on a beamy craft like the *Columbia* or *Constitution* cannot be stayed without the aid of spreaders. Or when a spreader succumbs to a gentle puff of wind without any real weight in it the mast itself should behave as an elongated tomato can or flimsy stove pipe might be expected to conduct itself under sudden stress, the mast head shrouds are supposed to be strong enough to support the mast in just such a crisis, there is no real need of a lower spreader at all. The narrow-gutted English cutters never carried these. Why should a craft of great beam like the *Constitution*, with ample spread to set up the lower rigging, risk the safety of a mast to a spreader that may snap short off like a rotten twig on the slightest provocation?

If Sir Thomas Lipton is successful in his attempt to "lift" the America's Cup, Yankees may find the blow easier to hear from the fact that the form of *Shamrock II* is modeled after that of *Columbia*—the victor in the Cup races of 1899. Far more artistic and pleasing to the eye, with "sweeter" and fairer lines and curves than that marvelous creation of Nat Herreshoff. [The] *Shamrock II* possesses the intrinsic merits from which *Columbia* derived her extraordinary speed and splendid all-round qualities. When Mr. Herreshoff built the *Columbia* he seemed to devote all his talent to perfecting the shape of the yacht below the water line—the part of the hull, which wins Cups. He wasted no time in making her topsides beautiful to look upon. He cared not a snap for a pleasing sheer or a graceful contour to the counter. However, his chief concern was devoted to turning out a fast and beautifully balanced craft that could render a good account of herself in any kind of weather—blow high, blow low. In this, he was remarkably successful.

If you compare the underbodies of the *Columbia* and *Shamrock II*, you cannot fail to be impressed with the wonderful points of resemblance. Neither can you refrain from congratulating Mr. George L. Watson on his gift of knowing a good thing when he sees it, and for his skill in putting a beautiful top on an already beautiful and thoroughly tested bottom. Side by side afloat, the *Columbia* looks crude when contrasted with *Shamrock II*. She appears

The NYYC contracted Herreshoff to design and build the Cup Defender *Constitution*, for the 1901 contest. During the summer of 1901, the *Constitution* had six trial races with the *Independence* and the previous defender the *Columbia*.

to have been finished in a hurry. In a word, she looks like an ugly duckling beside her swan-like rival, the latest challenger. Still the *Columbia* has a host of admirers who are prepared to wager heavily that the champion of 1899 is capable of beating this new Watson boat handsomely. The *Columbia* is now in magnificent shape, highly tuned up, skillfully handled. Better than ever she was, in fact, as her battles with the *Constitution* show.

It must be a matter of unalloyed regret to the friends of Mr. Watson that the eminent naval architect had no opportunity of seeing the *Constitution* before he designed the present challenger. This, of course, was a physical impossibility to the ordinary human being, and Mr. Watson is no warlock. But if by some magic art he could have studied the hull of the *Constitution* with the same care as he did that of *Colombia*, and with the same practical result, I, for one, should regard the America's Cup as in peril. What I mean is if to the underbody of the *Constitution* were added the topsides and the rig of *Shamrock II*, then we would have to meet a most formidable foe. But as it is there is no cause for alarm.

Jack doesn't mind whether a bridge-builder or a ship-builder puts the hull together. He however reserves the right of his own opinion regarding telescopic top-masts and spreaders for the lower rigging. Mr. Watson, after the dismasting of *Shamrock II*, on the memorable occasion when King Edward was aboard, constructed a new steel spar combining lower-mast and top-mast. He took a bamboo for his guide—one of the lightest and strongest productions of nature. In this, he has the advantage of Mr. Herreshoff. The occasions are so rare, indeed, when a ninety-footer ought really to house her top-mast that a spar incapable of being housed can scarcely be regarded as defective. The telescoping top-mast weakens the lower-mast inasmuch as it does not permit the lower masthead to be fitted with the usual strengthening diaphragms and flanges that add so much to its stability.

Personally, I believe that *Shamrock II* is not quite good enough to capture the America's Cup except by a fluke or an accident to the Yankee boat. The Herreshoff model is superb, though it may lack the artistic curves of Mr. Watson above the water line. It would be galling in the extreme to our national pride if Sir Thomas Lipton should "lift" the Cup because some wretched spreader or dolphin-striker collapsed at a critical moment on the defending boat. It seems to me, however, that only by a fluke or a mishap can he win this year.

CHAPTER ELEVEN

1901, Shamrock II vs. Columbia

AFTER DUNRAVEN'S EXTRAORDINARY BAD behavior which led to his ejection from the New York Yacht Club, Commodore Pierpont Morgan was so taken by Lipton's extraordinary good sportsmanship that he proposed him for honorary membership in the club.

Lipton's second challenge came about one year later. On October 2, 1900, the New York Yacht Club received Lipton's official challenge.

Two years after the challenge, William Watson created the *Shamrock II*. Watson tried to produce a yacht with the essential features of the American racers, but his work was largely experimental. Before this, the typical English racing cutter was a long, narrow, deep vessel. She kept from rolling over by an immense weight of lead bolted to her keel. She was slow in light air because she had so much body under water and so little sail above. She was fast and could go smartly about her business in a choppy blow.

Off Sandy Hook during the yachting season, there are seldom heavy winds or rough seas. Moderate to brisk winds prevail, and the sea is smooth, or runs in long swells. It was for such conditions as these that the American yachts of those early days were designed.

The problems before designers of racing yachts are the increase of sail carrying power and the decrease of the resistance of the hull in passing through the water. Sail carrying power is obtained, first, by giving a yacht plenty of beam. It is increased by giving her depth and placing the ballast at the lowest point. Resistance to the water is diminished by making that part of the vessel, which is under water as small as possible. To accomplish these designers cut away the forward part of the underbody of their vessels so that the whole bow is nothing by a long, narrow blade. Then they raise the bilge, the shoulder formed at the point where the inward and downward curve of the side begins, as high as possible. A deep keel, with some ninety tons of lead at its extreme lower edge completes the design.

THE CONTENDERS

The *Independence*

In Boston, Designer B. B. Crowninshield busied himself with construction of a new potential Cup defender called the *Independence* by owner Thomas W. Lawson.

In contrast to the secrecy, which previously surrounded the design and construction of challenging and defending yachts on their respective sides of the ocean, the 90-foot yacht the *Independence's* working drawings and photographs of construction details were published in widely circulating scientific and yachting magazines.

The widely published dimensions of the *Independence* are these: Length over all, 140 feet 10½ inches; length on water line, 90 feet; overhang forward, 27 feet 5½ inches; overhang aft, 23 feet 5 inches; beam, extreme, 23 feet 11½ inches; beam at water line, 23 feet 5 inches; draft extreme, 2 feet; freeboard at stemhead, 6 feet 11 inches; freeboard at taffrail 4 feet 8 inches; freeboard, least, 4 feet; deck beam at forward end of water line, 15 feet; deck beam at after end of water line, 18 feet 9 inches; beam at tafffrail, 11 feet 8 inches; area of lateral plane, 772.6 feet; area of midship section, 117.9 feet; area of load waterline plane, 1,771.5 feet; wetted surface, with small rudder, 2,913.5 feet; with large rudder, 2,956 feet; displacement, 146.75 tons.

These characteristics of the *Independence* are her extremely long overhangs, giving her an overall length fully ten feet greater than that of any previous Cup defender. Coupled with this great length is the fact that she carries her hard bilges and flat floor well out beyond the normal 90-foot mark, both forward and aft, thus providing an extremely long, flat floor and a great gain in water line length when heeling. With this form of hull, it is possible to carry a maximum amount of sail with a minimum amount of ballast; she will carry only 75 tons of lead in her keel as against the 85 to 90 tons, which are generally credited to the *Defender* and the *Columbia*.

The 1901 Cup Defender contender,
the sloop *Independence*.

The best idea of the full bow and stern sections and natural sail-carrying power of the Independence is seen in the photographic views of the
interior of the hull looking toward the bow and toward the stern from
the mast-step. Here is seen how the flat floor extends almost the entire
length of the yacht, the hard curves at the bilges are maintained will into
the bow, and carried out to the last rib.

There is a bluffness in the bow which the lines of the yacht will be such
as not merely to provide great sail-carrying power, but which will garner
itself to great speed. The designer believes that when she is driven to the
extreme, she should leave a delightfully smooth wake.

Another interesting provision is made for giving the necessary longitudinal strength to the long, overhang bow, and stern. A deep, vertical
keel-plate varies from a depth of 9 inches at the bow to 18 inches at the
point where the fin keel begins. At the center line of the deck there is also

To view the photographic images mentioned here, see *The America's Cup Yachts: The Rhode Island
Connection*, Arcadia Publishing, 1999.

a horizontal steel plate of 18 inches associated with the vertical plate that is from 6 to 8 inches in depth. Between these two plates, there is a system of tie rod braces and vertical, hollow, steel struts, the rods varying from seven-eighths of an inch to one inch in diameter and the struts from one and a half inches to two inches in diameter. This construction provides a deep steel truss extending from the stiffened framing at the mast out to the end of the overhanging bow.

The author of the detailed *Scientific American* article goes on to postulate that:

> There can be no question of the great originality and skill which the construction of this interesting boat has been worked out. The peculiarly of her form, her great sail-carrying capacity, involve that she will put to severer strains than any yacht of her size that has yet been launched; and we think the designer is to be congratulated upon the success of which he has combined lightness and strength in producing a powerful form. Had the *Independence* been built upon what might be called the commonly accepted lines of a 90-footer, and had there been less originality shown in the design, there would not be the great public interest attending her trials against the Herreshoff boat which is now certain to be manifest.

The *Constitution*

Assuming that the new Nat Herreshoff defender is an improved *Columbia*, as the *Columbia* was an improved *Defender*, it is interesting, with the plans of the Lawson boat, we can compare the points of difference between the *Independence* and the *Columbia*. First, comparing the *Independence's* midship section it has a harder bilge, a flatter floor and the curve at the garboards is of much smaller radius; in these respects, she is not unlike the *Shamrock*. Leaving the midship section, the difference between the *Independence* and the *Columbia* becomes obvious. In the *Columbia* the bilges begin to ease away rapidly toward the bow until at the forward end of the water line the cross section of the bow approximates a blunt V shape, thus giving a sharp and easy entrance and water lines that do not lengthen much as the boat heels to a breeze. Aft of midship the run and

Capt. Nat's *Constitution* built for
W. Butler Duncan, Jr., syndicate is
an improved *Columbia*.

quarters of the *Columbia* are remarkably fine and easy, and although in
a breeze, she lengthens her water line almost to the taff-rail. The form is
such that there is but little perceptible drag, or quartering wave, when
the vessel is reaching in a strong breeze.

The *Constitution* is a high powered *Columbia*, with the same sheer plan,
the same draft, a lighter hull, more lead, with exactly one-foot more beam,
with a dead-rise, a flatter floor, and a harder bilge. Because of these combined improvements, and carrying about 1,300 more square feet of canvas
than the *Columbia* the one objective of increased power is accomplished.

All things being equal the paramount object aimed at in the design of a
90-foot racing yacht is power, or the ability to carry a maximum amount
of sail. This is secured by changes in form or by reduction of weight or
both. Increased power due to form is gained by decrease of beam, by
flattening the floor and hardening or filling out the bilges, thereby raising
the buoyancy and placing the body of the boat more on the surface of the
water. Power due to form, however, is gained at the expense of sweetness.

It is the genius of the designer who finds that happy medium which gives a maximum power with a minimum hardness of form. Here, we can evaluate the development of Herreshoff's last three boats. In the *Defender*, her midship section is the sweetest and most beautiful form ever seen in an American 90-footer. Her bilges are rounded in to the reverse curve of the garboards with the unbroken sweep of the letter 'S'.

In the *Columbia*, her floor is flatter, her beam is increased, her bilge hardens, and the garboard curve is reduced.

In Herreshoff's new creation, the *Constitution*, he pushed development still further; there is even less dead rise, there is a distinctly straight line in the floor, and the bilge is still harder than that of the *Columbia*. The results of this development, in terms of sail area are seen in the respective figures of 12,640 square feet for *Defender*, 13,125 for *Columbia*, and 14,400 for *Constitution*.

To provide the required strength at the mast-step, which is twenty inches further aft than the *Columbia's* mast, an extra belt-rib is introduced, there being a belt-rib at stations 28, 30, and 32. The web of the ribs also increased to seven fortieths of an inch. The step is formed by a combination of these ribs with a deep keelson of seven sixteenths of an inch steel worked intercostally between the ribs, from station 24 to station 36, the keel plate being increased to five eighths of an inch in thickness beneath the mast and for the full length of the mast-step. The keelson increases in depth from rib 24 to rib 28.

The mast framing at the deck is stiffened against fore-and-aft racking strains by a trussing of hollow steel tubing, which extends in a fore-and aft plane from the deck beam to the over plate of the keelson. Three-inch tubular bilge struts extend from all the belt frames at the bile to the same ribs at the deck; but in wake of the most these struts are moved in to further assist in bracing the mast-ring and mast-step construction. The whole design is entirely novel, and shows the characteristic resourcefulness of Bristol's Capt. Nat Herreshoff.

From what was learned of the lowering of the *Constitution's* weight and the increased power of her form, it was evident that she could hoist aloft a spread of sail that rival that of the *Independence* in square surface of canvas. Compared with the *Columbia*, the boom was lengthened to 110 feet, about four feet added to the hoist, the fore triangle was lengthened, and as well, the topmast and gaff, with the result of a total of 14,400 square feet of sail was carried.

THE *SHAMROCK II*

Before deciding to accept Sir Tom's commission to design his second America's Cup challenger, Mr. G. M. Watson enlisted the aid of the Denny Brothers Shipyard in Dumbarton. At the time, the Dennys were noted as the most scientific of Scottish boat builders. Watson called on the Dennys to carry out an exhaustive series of experiments in their test tank, reputed as one of the most fully equipped test tanks in Britain.

The experiments began in June 1900 and continued for nine months before Mr. Watson was satisfied he had sufficient data to proceed in designing a Cup challenger. During the course of the tank tests, eleven models of the proposed racer were made and no fewer than sixty modifications were made. William Fife, Jr., designer of the first *Shamrock* lent a willing hand in this part of the work. The same test tank was used to evaluate the qualities of *Shamrock I* and the *Valkyrie III* one against the other and to test them fully against the qualities of the new racer under consideration.

The anonymous author of the May 11, 1901 *Scientific American* article about the *Shamrock II* described Lipton's new racer as:

> . . . a boat of the ordinary type with a shallow canoe-like body steadied by a deep bulbed keel under water and drawn out into long, sharp ends above.

The writer observing construction of the new yacht said it is thought to be a throwback to the old, so-called "cod-head and mackerel-tail" type favored by designers who worked before mathematics entered yacht designing:

> The bow lines of the new challenger carry the beam further into the forward overhang than has any racing yacht previously built in Britain. In the after body, the description of a fish tail is justified because the quarters and counter are drawn to a finer point than has ever been attempted in a yacht this size built on either side of the Atlantic.

The point of extreme beam is forward of the mast, its width is certainly not under 24 feet, but the drawing in of the after body is so thoroughly done that the long counter is tipped with a taff-rail which measures about six or seven feet across.

Considering that American boats of this size and complexity have generally been fuller in the bow than those built by the British, it is a fair conclusion to say the *Shamrock II* is incorporating American ideas and carrying them to an extreme.

The writer concludes from his observations:

To the eye trained to the ordinary type, it looks as though the new challenger may be lacking in power in the after body, but it is unlikely that Watson adopted a change of this nature without first assuring himself of its value.

These are the most striking characteristics of the *Shamrock II*; however, there are other features less noticeable but still worthy of attention. The underside of the forward overhang is beautifully formed, with sections which give almost perfect segments of a circle. Under the bow, the shape is exactly that of the forward end of a soup spoon, and this shape, together with the great beam, gives the impression of a yacht which has little danger of developing the great fault of *Shamrock I*, that of burying her head when being driven hard.

In her sections . . . she is noteworthy for the easy curves of her bilges and garboards; she is easier than both *Shamrock I* and even the *Columbia*. The floor has a fair amount of dead rise, and the turn where the fin and the hull join is also sweet and easy. In drawing the big deck plan down into the small underbody there was a danger of making some hard and awkward turnings, but this has been successfully avoided; the yacht shows fair, true lines of much beauty.

The boat's framing is bulb nickel steel and the plating from keel to rail is manganese bronze. Experimenting with spars begin before Cup racing trim is finally settled on; the mast was stepped immediately after launch, it is a hollow steel stick built as to allow a wooden topmast telescoping inside. The boom and gaff are of the same construction, and lightness has been pushed so far that the gaff is built of plates only three sixteenths of an inch thick. To save additional weight, and for convenience of construction the bow has been snubbed off, giving it an unusually peculiar appearance.

Sir Tom's 1901 challenger
the *Shamrock II*, she proved
not to be as powerful a sailor
as the 1899 *Shamrock*.

Members of the British yachting fraternity, gentlemen of considerable good judgment mused loudly that the *Shamrock II* is undoubtedly the most beautifully-lined challenger ever built, and though there is a possibility that she may sail a little tender in fresh winds, the hull carries with it the suggestion that she will be a dangerous opponent in anything less than moderate winds.

THE 1901 CONTENDERS

One has only to glance at the pod of 1901-Cup yachts and the table of their measurements to be convinced that in the effort to produce, on a specific waterline length, the fastest possible sail-driven racer the designers arrived at a common type from which they vary only in minor details.

	LENGTH OVER ALL FT. INCH	BEAM FT. INCH	DRAFT FT. INCH	BALLAST TONS	SAIL AREA SQ. FT.
Shamrock II	135 0	25 0	19 0	95	14,200
Constitution	132 6	25 2½	19 10	93	14,400
Independence	140 10½	23 11½	20 0	75	14,300

The plan for originality of a one-type yacht, as far as the modeling of the hull is concerned, belongs to the young Boston designer, B.B. Crown-inshield,[12] who in modeling his first 90-footer, the *Independence*, has not hesitated to branch out on new and previously untried lines. However, the most original boat of the three is Herreshoff's *Constitution* which differs so widely in this respect from her competitors and from all other 90-foot racing yachts that have preceded her, that she stands in a class entirely her own.

Of the Watson yacht, this is similar to his *Sybarita* design, which proved the fastest 90-foot yacht in British waters. The *Shamrock II* differs from that boat chiefly in her bow sections, the overhang being much longer and the beam carried much further into the bow, with a substitution of flat and full sections for the sharper V-sections, which are found in the bow of the *Sybarita* and other Watson designs. In construction, she is not unlike the *Shamrock I* with the difference that her sheer strake is of steel instead of aluminum.

Contemporary sport writers declared that when the three competing yachts are seen going through their paces under sail their performance might be described as "truly sensational."

As trained observers of their craft, sport writers are at times astute prognosticators of the results of clashing opposing teams. In this case, the unidentified *Scientific American* sport writer predicts the result of the 1901-Cup challenge:

Shamrock II, after her defeat by *Shamrock I* [during the shakedown trials in the Ettrick Bay, Isle of Bute, Scotland], appears to have very little prospect of winning the Cup. The only element of uncertainty, as far as she is concerned, hinges of the possibility that *Shamrock I* is sailing faster than she was when over here in 1899; but inasmuch as orders were given that, to render her a medium of comparison, the older vessel should not be changed, we see no reason to suppose that she is a faster boat now than then.

As to the speed of the *Constitution* and the *Independence* there has been no scale by which to judge. Nevertheless, we should be greatly surprised if both of these boats are not faster than the *Columbia*, and this for two reasons. In the first place, the *Constitution* is several tons lighter in construction than the *Columbia*, and by transferring the weight so saved from the hull to the keel, and adding 12 inches to her beam, it has been possible to increase her sail-plan at least 10 percent over that of the *Columbia* without giving her more displacement than that boat.

The *Independence*, on the other hand, has achieved the same result by the peculiarity of her model. Although her hull is probably no lighter than that of the *Columbia*, she gains power through the flattening of the floor and hardening of the bilges, and the carrying of the floor out into overhangs of exceptional length. As originally designed, she was to carry a sail-spread of 14,611 square feet, with a total amount of ballast of 75 tons. The unprecedented character of her model—unprecedented, that is, for a 90-footer—rendered this tentative method of proportioning the spars almost a necessity; and, very wisely, care was taken to have the sail-spread over rather than under the capacity of the boat.

The enormous sail-plans, the fact that the designers have kept down the factor of safety to the vanishing point, and the possibility of piping breezes during the month of September, when the races will be held, introduce elements of uncertainty which may yet land the Cup in the lockers of the boat which carries the stoutest spars and gear.

[The] *Independence* was sailing early in June. I must say that when I saw the picture of the *Independence* I thought my father's Cup boats would be beaten by *Independence*, but things turned out quite differently for she had structural trouble and leaked badly; she did not steer well, and her very flat model had so much wetted surface that she was very dull in light weather.

—L. Francis Herreshoff

TRIAL RACES

Constitution vs. *Columbia*

A series of mishaps to the sister yachts marred the beginning to the trial races.

On the first leg of the first race, the *Constitution* pulled the clew out of her jib; before a new jib was set the *Columbia* had a substantial lead and sprinted to the finish winning easily with time allowance.

In the second race, the *Columbia* broke down; her bobstay spreader, or martingale bent severely and skipper Charlie Barr lowered sail to prevent other parts from collapsing.

The next race, on July 6, was a windward and leeward race of fifteen miles to a leg in a light easterly breeze with a rolling sea. The *Constitution* sailed well to windward reaching and running, beating *Columbia* by some ten minutes corrected time.

On the New York Yacht Club cruise in the run from New London to Newport the *Constitution* struck bottom off Race Rock and retreated to Herreshoff's boatyard for repairs. During the summer, both yachts returned to the builder's yard for minor improvements including many new sails and sail modifications.

During the summer, the yachts sailed against each other twenty times, each winning nine and in the two matches that were called off for lack of wind the *Columbia* was leading. In every race, the yachts proved evenly matched owing to the sailing ability of the respective skippers. Choosing the defender proved a difficult decision for the Cup Committee, eventually the Committee chose the *Columbia* to meet the *Shamrock II*.

The *Columbia* vs. *Shamrock II*

Two years after her defeat of the *Shamrock*, Nathanael Herreshoff's *Columbia* built for J. Pierpont Morgan and Edwin Dennison Morgan and skippered by Charlie Barr, went on to defend the Cup again against the much newer *Shamrock II* in a best of five race series from September 28 to October 4, 1901. Again, three different courses were run, and once again, the results were *Columbia* over *Shamrock II* three wins to zero. The first race on September 28, 30-mile windward–leeward course from Sandy Hook Lightship, *Columbia* won by one minute and 20 seconds on corrected time. The second race on October 3, a 30-mile triangular course, *Columbia* whipped *Shamrock II* by three minutes and 45 seconds on corrected time. The third race on October 4, a 40-mile windward-leeward course, *Columbia* sank all hopes for a different outcome by defeating *Shamrock II* by 41 seconds on corrected time.

The *Columbia* made America's Cup history as the first boat to win the coveted Cup two times in succession. In 1903, the *Columbia* was refitted with the hope of being selected for a third defense; however, she was badly beaten in the selection trials by the *Reliance*.

Summary

At the close of the 1901 races, the results proved that the two antagonists came so closely together that the result was largely a question of the skill of seamanship and weather. Acknowledged by all that the designers had apparently reached the limit of their cleverness with the type of yacht employed for these contests. Mr. Herreshoff, in spite of all the rich store of knowledge acquired in the construction of four previous Cup defenders, had been unable in that year to produce a boat superior to his *Columbia*. While Mr. Watson in spite of the much talked-of test tank experiments was unable to beat the first *Shamrock* in her improved condition, by more than a very slight margin.

The *Columbia* hauled out at City Island, after the 1901 Cup races.

The *Constitution* hauled out at New London after the 1901 trial races.

Capt. Nat's champion *Columbia* distinguished herself as being the first sloop to defend the Cup in two successive races. She was cut up for scrap in 1913 at City Island, New York.

CHAPTER TWELVE

1903, *Shamrock III vs. Reliance*

In thus desiring an opportunity of making a third attempt to obtain possession of the America's Cup, I hope I may not be deemed impertinent or unduly covetous of the precious trophy so long and so securely held in trust by NYYC.

— Thomas J. Lipton letter to the New York Yacht Club.

T HE NECESSITY FOR BUILDING a new Cup defender was apparent when the challenge for the 1903 series of contests was received and accepted by the New York Yacht Club.

The supposed superiority of the *Constitution* to the *Columbia* was at very best hypothetical, based solely upon the presumably better handling than the *Columbia* had received during the trial races. At the same time, the Fife-built *Shamrock*, after some readjustment of her sail plan, had proved to be practically equal under many conditions of sailing to the Watson-designed *Shamrock II*. Fife received the commission to build the *Shamrock III*; general thought being that in all probability, he would succeed in turning out a craft faster than the two earlier *Shamrocks*.

The New York Yacht Club determined retention of the Cup depended upon building a new racer, and the task of designing the craft should be Herreshoff's.

THE CHALLENGE

For the twelfth time a vessel crosses the Atlantic in quest of the America's Cup.

The *Shamrock III* and a cartouche image of owner Thomas J. Lipton on a 1903 U.S. picture post card.

The old rule governing the passage of any challenger to the place of the races is that she must arrive "on her own bottom;" that Deed of Gift rule gives rise, in many quarters that such a sail of three thousand miles across the unpredictable Atlantic connotes a handicap. It is true that the challenging yacht must be built of sufficient strength to stand the stress of heavy seas, which she is liable to encounter in crossing to America. To give her this margin of strength she must be somewhat heavier scantling, and her plating must be of greater thickness, than is necessary in the case of the defending American yacht. The turbulent Atlantic Ocean puts a limit upon lightness of construction; it also puts a limit on exaggeration of form because no yacht of the scow-type like the *Independence* would risk the ocean passage. It was widely reported how her bow plates were stressed as she was being towed in a gale rounding Point Judith, Rhode Island, when the boat was in such a bad way that the question of her ability to race was raised.

When the *Independence* was hauled out at City Island a large number of rivets under the bow, and the butt joints of the plating were clearly defined by circles and lines of red rust. Since the plating and the rivets are of bronze, the rust could not have come from them, but must have worked through from the nickel-steel frames on the inside of the hull. It could only have come from the frames by virtue of the whole structure being severely "twisted" to allow salt water to seep through at the rivets.

How the *Reliance* would fare under similar conditions is one of the questions sport writers watching the defense of the Cup asked with some concern. They hoped the trials off Sandy Hook would furnish the desired test of her broad, flat bow. Her bow which while not so flat as the *Independence*, is still of such a very pronounced scow-type that as she swings round from tack to tack in a hammer to windward, the impact of the seas will be extreme and will prove a severe tax upon the light waterline framing and plating.

Sport writer Oliver Bronson Capen is author of the following article appearing in the August 1903, *Country Life in America* magazine:

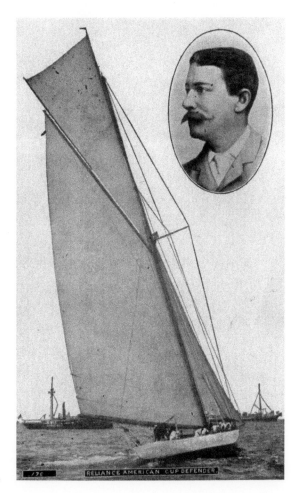

The Cup defender *Reliance* and a cartouche image of owner C. Oliver Iselin on a 1903 U.S. picture post card.

While the finial trials for the honor of defending the Cup will not begin until August 13, it seems almost certainly that the *Reliance* will be chosen. She has shown up superbly in almost every sort of sea in light and strong winds alike. She has beaten by over twenty minutes the record for a windward and leeward course of thirty miles. Granted her superiority to *Constitution* and *Columbia*, it is, however safe to say that this superiority is not as great as the recent race figures seem to show. She is better canvassed than the *Constitution*, and is managed by Captain [Charlie] Barr, while *Columbia* is sailed by an amateur—which makes a lot of difference. As for *Shamrock III*, she is reported to be much faster than *Shamrock I*, which is probably true; but it must be remembered that the same thing was said of *Shamrock II* in 1901—a statement that did not hold water. The *Reliance* is built, to a considerable extent, along the lines of Lawson's *Independence*. It is scow-shaped at both bow and stern, but does not pound the water in rough weather, as did the Boston boat. Her hull is broad and shallow, while that of *Shamrock III* is, comparatively speaking, narrow, and deep. The British yacht, like the *Reliance*, has a scow stern, but the bow is like the half of a cone that has been cut lengthwise.

This year's first round of races was scheduled for sailing on the Sandy Hook course on August 20. The wait between the arrival of the *Shamrock III* and the start of the matches caused increasing interest across the country. An added stimulus of interest is aroused because three fast American yachts are striving for the honor of defending the Cup.

Sir Thomas Lipton, the central figure in all the enthusiasm, came besieging with a small navy—his *Shamrock* yachts, I and III, each with a crew of more than forty, his steam yacht the *Erin* which is manned by fifty men, the sea-going tug the *Cruizer*, and two American built launches. Lipton resolutely made this third expedition with his one hundred sixty seamen endeavoring to snatch the old silver ewer from the New York Yacht Club.

In measurements alone, the third Lipton challenger stands out as distinct from any of the recent yachts, which have crossed the Atlantic to do battle with the American Cup defender. Until now, the challengers, with the possible exception of the Watson-built *Valkyrie III*, have followed a distinct line of development. The progress from one to the other could be easily traced, and the efforts made in each succeeding boat to make good

On this British real photograph post card the *Shamrock III* is seen testing her gear in the Ettrick Bay.

the apparent weaknesses of her predecessors were easily distinguishable. In the *Shamrock II's* bold bid in her contest with the *Colombia*, designer William Fife had a strong temptation to follow the same lines in *Shamrock III*. However, the new boat shows that he had chosen to return to some essential features to the model of the *Britannia* whose successful defeat of the *Vigilant*—when she sailed for a season in British waters—led to the use by Herreshoff of the *Britannia's* lines greatly refined in the *Defender*.

The result is that the *Shamrock III* while having the outstanding features that have characterized all the recent Cup races, possesses important developments, which may make her the most formidable of the latest series of challengers. In waterline length there is little to distinguish her from other vessels built expressly for Cup racing. It has long been a conviction with designers that the time allowance given for lack of waterline length does not put the shorter boat on a level with the yacht of greater length, and their desire is therefore to build as near the allowable limit of 90 feet as possible.

Both yachts are carrying an enormous spread of sail. It is not by whim or chance that these racing yachts are designed to raise so much canvas.

In fact, in the building of these vessels the effect of every square inch of sail is calculated with mathematical exactness. Many years of experience and a vast amount of experimentation have proved that the scow-shaped, comparatively broad, and shallow hull offers the least friction to the water. Nat Herreshoff, after studying the English idea, adopted elements of very deep keels loaded with lead, which balance the weight of the gigantic masts loaded with tons of sail, and the wind pressure against them. However, strength must be sacrificed to the benefit of speed; the towering steel masts of both the *Reliance* and the *Shamrock III* snapped during trials early in the season.

Contemporary reports put the cost of the *Reliance* in the neighborhood of thirty thousand dollars; tongue-wagging cynics voiced their diatribe saying that after the race, she "will be good for nothing but old junk." As one New York paper put it, "Herreshoff's latest monstrosity is a spar-deck between a bulb of lead and an acre of sail." Sport writer Oliver Bronson Capen continues:

> The racer of today is such a delicate creature that it is really a great risk to let her feet get wet. What the next turn of the screw in the development of ocean racing machines will lead to is an open question. It is hoped that common sense will once more come to the front and that real boats will again be pressed into service.

	SHAMROCK III	RELIANCE
Water Line Length	89.78	89.66
Length Over All	134.42	143.69
Beam	23.00	25.00
Draft	19.00	20.00
Spinnaker Boom Length	81.40	83.75
Forward point measurement to end of main boom	187.54	201.75
Measured Sail Area	14,154	16,159
Rating	104	108

THE *SHAMROCK III* IN DRYDOCK

When the *Shamrock III* revealed her underbody in drydock at the Erie Basin, it was evident that she corresponded very closely with the description furnished by *Scientific American*'s Glasgow correspondent at the time of her launch.

The Lipton racing yacht is a marked departure from any previous challenger that came over. We have to return to the *Valkyrie II* to find a midship section that has any similarity to the easy bilges and full garboards that distinguish the *Shamrock III* so sharply from any of her immediate predecessors, and in this respect, she is the most handsome of any of the existing challengers or defenders of the 90-foot class.

Fife designed a boat with remarkable extremes of beam, draft, and overall length in an attempt to carry a maximum amount of sail allowed under the rule. The overall length is close to 140 feet, the waterline length slightly under 90 feet; beam about 25 feet 6 inches; draft in racing trim is 21 feet and her displacement is in the neighborhood of 150 tons.

In the words of an unidentified *Scientific American* sport writer after contemplating her exposed quarters in drydock:

> Although her midship section is large, the lines, which have been carried out with the skill that characterizes all Fife boats, are so sweet and fair that she looks at first glance more like a 70-footer than a boat built up to the full 90-foot limit. The sections throughout are round and fair, free from sudden changes of curve or "humps", "round as a barrel" is a term that may justly be applied to *Shamrock III*. She should show small initial stability—a valuable feature when the wind is light and the sea troubled—while her deep and easy bilges will give her great sail-carrying power when she heels to her best sailing lines. The boat will be comfortable in a seaway, and she will do her best work over the windward and leeward course. Her deep midship section will be a drawback to the boat in reaching, especially when higher speeds are attained and wave making begins, and on this point of sailing *Reliance* will probably have no difficulty in leaving her. To windward, judged purely by their models, *Shamrock III*, should be the better boat; but *Reliance* has shown such unexpectedly good windward qualities that it is likely she will be able to hold on this point of sailing and possibly pull away from

her. Before the wind under spinnaker, *Shamrock III* because of her smaller wetted surface, should be the more slippery boat; but, on the other hand, the enormous sail plan of *Reliance* will probably outweigh her greater wetted surface, and pull her down to the leeward mark some minutes ahead of her more handsome sister.

The *Shamrock II's* sail plan was found to be so superior that it was adapted with very little change in the *Shamrock III*, the latter boat carrying about two-hundred more square feet of sail. The mast measured 158 feet, and the boom 104 feet, with a base line of 78 feet for the forward triangle. The rig, relatively to the *Reliance*, was narrow for its height and favorable for windward work. Contemporary observers questioned whether the deeper-bodied, rounder, and sweeter boat, with her generous sail plan of 14,400 square feet, could hold her own with a flat-floored, shoal, full-bowed boat, carrying 1,500 square feet more canvas.

At the time, the general sentiment of the ocean sailboat racing coalition was a clear case of a gamble on the weather, with the odds largely in favor of the overgrown *Reliance*. In winds that would allow the *Reliance* to carry her sail spread, the opinion is not a doubt to the outcome, but should the wind pipe up to a strength of 20 to 22 knots, they prophesize dire trouble for the scow and a good fighting chance for the smaller boat.

THE RELIANCE IN DRYDOCK

An unnamed *Scientific American* sport writer had these comments after witnessing the *Reliance's* launch and her subsequent reveal in drydock:

One of the most striking features in the *Reliance* is the long drawn out bow, which projects nearly thirty feet beyond the waterline. Only a small proportion of it can be utilized for gaining sailing length; for the *Independence* at thirty degrees heel only added five feet of length forward and she was even flatter than the *Reliance*. Driving into a head sea, she will take the seas a little earlier, but not so much earlier as to compensate, for the carrying of so much added bow weight at a height of eight or nine feet above the water. Many seasoned yachtsmen had wondered why the bow was not made shorter

Fresh out of Herreshoff's
construction shed, the *Reliance*
is on her shake-down cruise in
Narragansett Bay.

relatively to the stern. They wondered, knowing in a low, long stern such as that of *Reliance*, every foot of length can be utilized.

Even her designer admitted that the *Reliance* is something of an experiment however, and only an actual test in a jump of a sea off Newport or Sandy Hook can determine the value of such an extreme bow.

The problem for Herreshoff was to design a yacht with all the best features of the scow-type, such as great sailing length when heeled, and large sail-carrying power, with as few as possible of the scow's drawbacks, such as the flat floor forward and the hard shoulders, which was the undoing of the *Independence* in a troubled sea. This Herreshoff achieved in the model of the *Reliance*, although with what measure of success will be known only when the boat commences to sail on some calm Newport day with the leftover disturbance of the previous day's blow.

The new boat has more beam and considerably less dead rise than the *Constitution*, a harder bilge and longer ends, particularly in the forward overhang. Her extreme beam is 25 feet 8 inches, her draft is 18 feet 9 inches, and her length over all is 140 feet. In her midship section, she shows exactly 2 feet less dead rise than the *Constitution*, and while her hull is not as shallow as that of the *Independence*, it is still sufficiently shallow to allow the ends to be carried out to give practically the same length on deck as the *Independence*.

Although the draft is less than that of the *Constitution*, the keel is longer and the bulb is drawn out to finer lines. The mast relatively to the load water line is stepped in the same position as in the *Constitution*. With 100 tons of lead in her keel, her harder bilges, greater beam, and greater length of water line when heeled, she will naturally possess larger sail carrying power; her spread is in the neighborhood of 16,000 square feet of canvas.

THE RESULTS

In his third attempt at returning the Cup to Britain, Lipton came up against the super boat, the racing marvel called *Reliance*. Stretching a full 50 yards from the tip of her bowsprit to the end of her boom, Herreshoff's creation raised fully one-third of an acre of canvas, her hull constructed so light and so delicate that the fury of a tortured sea could dent her bow.

Sir Tom, when referring to his third attempt to win the Cup said, "You could not say I went into this hazard of challenging for the America's Cup on a hasty impulse." Speculation was that the *Shamrock III*, was much faster than the *Shamrock*, but it must be remembered that the same thing was said of *Shamrock II* in 1901—a statement that did not hold water. After people got a good look at *Shamrock III*, they began to believe she had a chance at victory.

The yachts eventually met in late August. The races by these giant sloops, with long overhang at bow and stern and their tremendous expanse of sail, must have been a thrill to witness. *Reliance* captured all three races. *Shamrock III* getting lost in fog withdrew during the third race; rather than finishing the race, she set her course for shore.

Contemporary sport writers universally agreed that the races were a disappointment, the *Reliance* not only won, but also won very easily. *Shamrock III* did not make nearly as good a showing as her predecessors.

The failure of the *Shamrock III* was attended by many laments of British as well as world sport writers. One particularly glib report, appeared in Lipton's hometown newspaper, *The Glasgow Town Topics*, authored by a writer using the *nom-de-plume* "The Horse-Marine"; his critique is presented below:

You may talk about Lipton as you will; you may deride his penchant for bussing soubrettes square on their mouths—especially you of mature years who have outgrown such luxurious habits—but no matter what you may accuse our Cup challenger of, you cannot say that he is anything but the most graceful loser we ever saw. He takes his defeat so pleasantly and grace-fully that none can help applauding, and while congratulating him on his successful [business] advertising, we can compliment him on his manhood and his sportsmanship.

There is nothing of the common scold about Sir Thomas. When you contrast his behavior with that of Lord Dunraven the dour, the sullen, and the sour, you are compelled to use generous adjectives and bless yourself that Dunraven is consigned to the limbo of dead dogs, while Lipton, of tea, jam, pork, and whiskey fame, is still with us and ready to challenge again when the fiat comes forth from the Regatta Committee that he has loved and lost once more.

To lose his third attempt without one single growl at the men who sold him a gold brick in the shape of the third Shamrock shows a squareness of principle that endears him to all. I, The Horse-Marine, offer him my most sincere, humble apologies for my flippant and envious talk about his girl conquests, and take off my hat to him as a true sportsman.

The "Resolute," with Spinnaker Set, Running before the Wind in the Second Trial Race

How the "Defiance" Appeared under Full Sail in the Greenwich Races

The "Vanitie" Setting the Balloon Jib to Overtake the "Resolute"

PHOTO COPYRIGHT. INTERNATIONAL NEWS SERVICE

PHOTO COPYRIGHT. UNDERWOOD & UNDERWOOD

A 1914 copy of Popular Mechanics published this page illustrating the three potential Cup Defenders: the *Resolute*, the *Defiance*, and the *Vanitie*. With the outbreak of World War I, the contest was postponed until 1920.

CHAPTER THIRTEEN

1920, Shamrock IV vs. Resolute

As might be expected, the launching of *Shamrock IV* by Lady Shaftesbury was admirably stage-managed. A hundred newspapermen travelled down in a specially decorated *Shamrock* train. A party of five hundred lunched in the [construction] shed; telegrams of well wishing arrived from the five continents and the seven seas. Lord Dewar presented a monkey as a mascot. It was the Queen's birthday, and the warships were dressed in Portsmouth Harbour, the old *Victory* firing a royal salute only a few minutes before *Shamrock* struck the water.

—— Alec Waugh, 1950

IN 1907, LIPTON ISSUED a conditional challenge. His condition was for a new measurement rule, which would take into account displacement as well as length and sail area. He withdrew his earlier challenge to race with a 75-footer and offered to meet the New York Yacht Club defender with a 90-foot boat.

Negotiations with the NYYC continued until 1912. Surprisingly, the committee accepted what they had previously refused, when both sides agreed to favor smaller and less-expensive yachts that had previously raced, Lipton challenged with his *Shamrock IV*, a 75-foot boat carrying 10,495 feet of sail. The Club accepted the challenge in May 1913 for a race in September 1914.

The *Shamrock IV* was on her way over to the scene of the match when the European war began. Lipton put in at Bermuda awaiting instructions. Later, he brought his yacht to New York where she was hauled out and stored for the duration of the war. The war resulted in the contest's cancellation; it did not occur until 1920.

The *Shamrock IV*, designed by Charles E. Nicholson, was not a very handsome craft, and even Nicholson referred to her as the "ugly duckling." Nicholson, the designer of several successful English yachts, had not previously designed a yacht to the specifications of the Universal Rule. Before building regulations became part of the measurement requirements, Nicholson endeavored to build an extremely light hull with a great deal of laminated wood.

She was a big boat that would have to hoist an enormous sail. Although she had a very high measurement rating for her waterline length of 75 feet, her final rating was over 94 feet. Above water, she was quite scow-shaped so that her lines were adapted to high speed, she had a snubbed nose, her bowsprit was not exceptionally long, her straight stem with her body squeezed in at the bulwarks, rounded outwards to the waistline going almost flat then tapering towards the keel and expanding outwards at the foot.

London newspaper reporter, Francis B. Cooke did not hesitate to describe her as a "freak." Despite her ascribed ugliness, she was thought to be a fast boat, and she would have to allow the defender a six-and-one-half-minute handicap.

June 15, 1914, The *Shamrock IV* starts on her trials in the Solent. In this period press photograph, Sir Tom (left) is seen resting on a spar, Sir William P. Burton is steering.

Lipton had his original 20-year old *Shamrock* sent to America to race against his new boat; several informal races were run to tune up the *Shamrock IV* to her peak performance.

DEFENDER CONTENDERS

The three yachts built for the defense included: the *Resolute*, a Herreshoff creation for a New York Yacht Club syndicate; the *Defiance*, designed by George Owen for Boston, New York and Philadelphia yachtsmen; and the *Vanitie*, by William Gardner, for Alexander S. Cochran, all just under a seventy-five-foot waterline.

Captain Nat Herreshoff had much experience building Cup defenders, while Owen, Gardner and Nicholson had never previously designed a boat to challenge for the Cup, nor did they enjoy the benefit as Herreshoff did of having use of his own construction company.

According to L. Francis Herreshoff, in the *Resolute*, Captain Nat made the diplomatic mistake of designing the craft to rate quite low, which was a great handicap to her. The reason he did this was that there had been much talk about the expense of Cup boats since the previous races in 1903 between the gigantic *Reliance* and *Shamrock III*, and he thought the best way to reduce cost was to design a small, low rating yacht.

When she came out, Herreshoff's *Resolute* was a nicely proportioned yacht with small sail area, but while the boat-to-boat finishes between her and *Vanitie* were often close, *Resolute*, as originally rigged, beat *Vanitie* quite easily with time allowance.

Listed below are the scores of the three defense contenders at the end of the first season of trials:

Resolute	15 firsts out of 18 starts
Vanitie	5 firsts out of 20 starts
Defiance	0 firsts out of 10 starts

For the 1915 series of defender trials, the *Resolute* afterguard convinced Mr. Herreshoff to give her more sail in order to increase her rating. Listed below are the scores at the end of the second season of trials:

Resolute	12 firsts out of 16 starts
Vanitie	4 firsts out of 16 starts

The *Defiance* withdrew after the 1914 trials. The committee selected the *Resolute* after a lively series with the *Vanitie* off Newport, Rhode Island.

THE RACE

The defender's crew was principally of Scandinavian birth. Some distinguished crewmembers of the Boston-owned and Boston-operated defender included: Chris Christensen who skippered *Resolute* with Charles Francis Adams at the wheel; manager, Robert W. Emmons; navigator, George Nichols, a son-in-law of J. P. Morgan, and famous Harvard footballer John Parkinson as a member of the afterdeck crew who would relieve Adams when the sloop ran downwind.

The *Shamrock's* crew was composed of Essex fishermen, as captain Lipton chose one of the best amateur skippers in England, Sir William P. Burton.

With amateur helmsman Burton, the *Shamrock* won the first of the five races by a stroke of luck. After a bad start and being well behind, the *Resolute* worked to windward of the challenger making better tactical decisions. Approaching the finish line, it looked like the defender would sprint to victory, suddenly the *Resolute's* throat halyards for the mainsail gaff parted at the below deck winch and the great mainsail came plummeting down. Thus, the challenger sailed past and crossed the finish line ahead of the defender.

Lipton did not want to win because of equipment failure on the defending yacht. He considered offering to cancel the race result, but friends with him aboard the *Erin* overruled him.

On July 15, the second race got off in a light breeze, the *Resolute* out sailed the *Shamrock IV* but the finish was not reached before the allotted time had elapsed consequently the race was called off.

In a replay of the second race, on July 20, the *Shamrock IV* won by 2-minutes 26-seconds corrected time, and finally, for the first time Lipton

The *Shamrock IV* sailing past the committee's observation boat. Image is from a period stereo view card.

could rejoice, in a real challenging race he had seen his green-colored cutter cross the finishing line ahead of a defender.

> A slight wind shift favorable to the English allowed them to merely grind in sheets a bit and fetch the mark but Adams could not point with the English on the new slant. The wind shifted a second time and *Shamrock* got ahead, never to lose her lead, thus beating the defender for the second race in a row.
>
> —— Geoffrey F. Hammond, 1974

Hammond writes in his *Showdown at Newport:*

> This was the first time in 69 years of America's Cup history that a defender had been beaten when she was not disabled. Defenders had been defeated only four times and Adams owned half of those defeats.

With the third and possibly final race scheduled, Nat Herreshoff rushed to New York overnight on a U.S. Navy destroyer to aid in saving the Cup. He and Adams worked feverishly making adjustments to the *Resolute's* rig, which freed the potential power in Herreshoff's design.

The third race got off on July 21; a great deal of interest circulated among those of the yachting fraternity as well as the general public because of the *Shamrock's* potential of capturing the Cup with a third win. The third race, certainly highly anticipated by Lipton, ended as the closest race in Cup history.

Negotiating 19 tacks on the windward-leeward course, the *Resolute* held the lead. The *Shamrock IV* fought back and the opponents finished in a dead heat, both covering the course in exactly the same elapsed time. However, because the challenger had given the defender a 7-minute 39-second handicap allowance, *Resolute* was the winner 7-minutes 1-second corrected time thus turning the odds in favor of the defender.

In the fourth race on a triangular course, skipper Sir William Burton succeeded in taking the *Shamrock IV* over the starting line with a 23-second lead. On the first leg to the windward, the *Shamrock IV* endeavored to go as high as the defender, but the *Resolute* kept racing ahead until she had the weather berth. On the next leg, a strong breeze arose and both yachts covered the ten miles at a speed of about 12-knots, at the second mark the defender had a one-minute 23-second lead. On the run home, in a fortunate puff of new air the challenger caught up and squeaked ahead of the defender; however, the wind swung to the south allowing the *Resolute* to set her ballooner and tack to the lee. Now, racing at a speedy clip she crossed the finish line 3-minutes 14-seconds ahead of the *Shamrock IV*.

The yachts now score two wins each.

The last race got off on July 27 in very light weather with the *Resolute's* 72-year old designer Nat Herreshoff aboard. Capt. Nat's son L. Francis Herreshoff witnessed the final race from the deck of a U.S.N. destroyer detailed to the NYYC for members and friends to witness the races.

The following quote is an abridgement of Francis Herreshoff's observations of the final struggle in the 1930 defense:

The fifth race was to be sailed, there was a smoky southwester developing, and I should think the regatta committee should have stayed in port and not attempted a race, but the committee boat and the two racers went to the starting line. *Resolute* went under jib and mainsail, and *Shamrock IV* under reefed mainsail, working topsail and jib. Shortly before starting time, the regatta committee called the race off much to the relief of both yacht crews for there was a near panic aboard the challenger, cause as follows: *Shamrock IV* was built with some deep web frames in her bow; I suppose to stand the heavy pounding that her flat bow might receive in a choppy sea. At the time we speak of a sail hatch was off in the forward deck and in maneuvering around … she had stuck her nose under [water] slightly a couple of times so that quite a little water was gathered in the deep bay under the hatch. When a deck hand went forward, he sang out, "She is leaking forward." [Later] they found out she was not leaking at all.

On July 27, the last race started in very light weather. The starting line was in a calm because of lack of wind. The usual afternoon southwest wind came in with strength enough for a start. Both yachts held back for the two-minute handicap gun and crossed the line at two-seventeen. The challenger seemed to slip along quite as well as the defender, but the latter somehow appeared to be working windward of her so that after a while, with their cross tacking, Adams brought *Resolute* about almost dead to windward of the challenger. From then on the challenger gradually dropped back so that at the weather mark she was four minutes and seven seconds behind. After rounding the weather mark neither yacht laid a course toward the finish line for *Resolute* tacked to leeward with a balloon jib set probably because Mr. Herreshoff could give them the proper course to take as he had been working on the problem of tacking to leeward for many years.

As the *Resolute* was tacking downwind, it was easy for her to occasionally keep between her competitor and the finish line. *Resolute* evidently made quite a gain in tacking to leeward for the yachts certainly seemed to be far apart near the finish, but as they were now going at a good clip she only beat *Shamrock IV* about twenty minutes corrected time.

This long drawn-out series of races had lasted twelve days; the result of these exciting races was Sir Tom's fourth loss to the Cup defender, 3–2.

Over the span of years, sport writers on both sides of the Atlantic generally admit that *Shamrock II* was the better of Lipton's challengers, but the *Shamrock IV* came closest to victory. Odds makers were betting that if the green yacht could catch the defender on a broad reach in a strong breeze of fifteen to twenty-five knots, she would surely out run her opponent, and Sir Tom could use that special-made box to ship the Cup back to England.

The *Enterprise* and owner-skipper Harold S. Vanderbilt Whip
Shamrock V to successfully defend the Cup. October 4, 1930
photograph from, The Literary Digest.

CHAPTER FOURTEEN

1930, Shamrock V vs. Enterprise

THE J BOAT ERA

Aﬅer Lipton's fourth defeat, nearly a decade passed before the New York Yacht Club received another challenge. An important agreement reached in 1930 by all seafaring nations with a potential interest in challenging for the Cup made significant changes in marine architecture and rating of yachts, and the introduction of multiple classes of yachts was established.

Lipton's last attempt to win the Old Mug signaled the end of an epoch as far as boat design is concerned. The *Shamrock V* is a near-replica of the 1930 defender, the J-boat *Enterprise*.

J-boats are long, beautiful sloops between 120 and 135 feet in overall length, with a waterline of at least 65 feet. These are smaller than previous Cup racers. The reason for this is that if size is reduced, more boats can participate. If more take part, there is a better chance of getting better challengers.

The America's Cup competition adapted the J-class in 1928, considering the 1930 regatta. The class itself, though, dates back to the turn of the century at the time of international acceptance of the Universal Rule. J-class yachts were the largest constructed under the Universal Rule. Only ten J-class yachts were designed and built. However, several yachts of closely related dimensions, mostly twenty-three-meter International Rule boats, converted to J-class after their construction to meet the rating rules.

Sir Tom built the *Shamrock V* in 1930 for his fifth and last attempt to wrench the America's Cup from the halls of the New York Yacht Club. This challenger was the first British yacht built to the new J-class Rule and the last of the J's built entirely of wood. After launch, she was continually

The J class *Weetamoe*, in her tuning up spins. She took the second race in the defender trials. Insert: the crew is sending up the mainsail.

upgraded with changes to her hull and rudder. Her rig was modified to create the most efficient racing sail plan; but alas, she was no match for the faster *Enterprise*.

CHOOSING THE DEFENDER

Following a precedent of long standing, the first move for the defense of the Cup was made by the flag officers of the club in the organization of two syndicates, one headed by Vice Commodore Winthrop W. Aldrich and the other by Rear Commodore Junius S. Morgan, Jr. Two additional defender syndicate managers, John S. Lawrence, and Paul Hammond followed these.

YACHT	DESIGNER	BUILDER
J1 Weetamoe	Clinton H. Crane	Herreshoff Mfg. Co.
J2 Yankee	Frank C. Paine	George Lawley & Son
J3 Whirlwind	L. Francis Herreshoff	George Lawley & Son
J4 Enterprise	W. Starling Burgess	Herreshoff Mfg. Co.

Clinton H. Crane, began his work as an amateur designer in 1894, the same year he graduated from Harvard. In 1896, he designed and raced his fifteen-footer, the *El Heirie*, in defense of the Seawanhaka International Trophy for small yachts. After a steady of naval architecture at the University of Glasgow, he returned to New York and for many years was associated with the firm of Tams, LeMoine & Crane, designing sail, and power yachts.

Frank C. Paine is the youngest son of Gen. Charles J. Paine, so prominently associated with Edward Burgess in the defense of the Cup in 1885, '86, and '87. Young Paine is a graduate of the Harvard class of 1912. His interest in sailing beginning as a youth led him to study yacht designing achieving remarkable success in the field.

W. Starling Burgess, elder son of Edward Burgess, designer of the *Puritan*, *Mayflower*, and *Volunteer*, graduated from Harvard in 1901, and followed a career of designing sailing yachts.

L. Francis Herreshoff, fifth son of Nathanael Green Herreshoff; brought up in the Herreshoff Mfg. Co. shipyard in Bristol, RI, he devoted himself to yacht designing and writing books on the subject of sail-powered yachts.

In the *Whirlwind*, as in the forty-six-foot *Istalena*, Francis Herreshoff has adhered to the conventional profile of his father's yachts, such as *Resolute*. The sternpost has a moderate rake; the keel is straight and long, and almost parallel with the line of keel almost straight from the heel of the sternpost to the fore end of the waterline.

Next in order to the deep, straight keel of the *Whirlwind* comes the *Enterprise*, with a profile resembling the Burgess ten and twelve-meter yachts, a rather short keel, slightly curved on the bottom and rising as it sweeps into a convex curve and then a concave to the water line.

The *Yankee* comes between the *Enterprise* and the *Weetamoe* in a moderate reverse curve upward from the heel of the post to the water line at the bow. With reduced lateral plane, a high center of gravity for her lead, and no effective centerboard, the *Yankee* may need all the ballast that the rule permits for both stability and lateral resistance.

With the extra foot of draft due to her long water line and low straight keel, *Whirlwind* leads in the important points of stability and lateral resistance. The *Enterprise*, next in place, in her resemblance to such proven yachts as the *Prestige* and the *Avatar*, presumably has all necessary stability, but may be happy to use her centerboard at times on the wind.

DEFENDER TRIALS

The selection trials for the yacht to be crowned Cup Defender were sailed on the NYYC course on August 20. Lipton and his *Shamrock V* managers watched the competition from the deck of his steam yacht the *Erin*.

In a light breeze, ranging from 6 to 12 knots, the *Enterprise* won the first of the trial races. The next day the wind increased blowing from the northeast at about 25 knots, again, the *Enterprise* crossed the finish line first beating the *Weetamoe* by 3 minutes. The *Enterprise* designer W. Starling Burgess saved the *Enterprise's* position as defender during the 1930 preliminary race against the *Weetamoe*.

Notably, that day the *Yankee* set a new record for the Club course of 2 hours, 47 minutes, 59 seconds racing against the *Whirlwind*; notwithstanding the selection committee chose the *Enterprise* as Cup Defender on the result of her great tally of win records for the season.

During the season, preceding the Cup Defender trials Harold Vanderbilt competed in three matches guiding his 121-foot J-class *Enterprise* and winning them all.

Harold S. Vanderbilt sailed to the pinnacle of yacht racing success by defending the America's Cup in his J-class yacht the *Enterprise* defeating Thomas J. Lipton's *Shamrock V.*

THE *ENTERPRISE*

The Starling Burgess-designed and Herreshoff-built 1930-Cup defender, the *Enterprise*, was the first to use the twelve-sided aluminum mast and a triangular boom, the so-called Park Avenue boom.[13] Other innovations included Tobin bronze plating; a triple-headed rig, trialed with retracting spreaders; a waterline length of 80 feet; and an overall length of 121 feet. Innovation in the boom enabled the mainsail to slide from one side to another and take in more breezes. A circular-sectioned double-skin duralumin mast built by the G. L. Martin Company replaced the original spruce mast; because of the innovative mast design, the *Enterprise* needed less ballast than the *Shamrock*. Captain Nicholson described the Burgess mast as the greatest engineering development in the history of the large, ocean racing yacht.

The Aldrich syndicate—Harold Vanderbilt, Vincent Astor, George Baker, George Whitney, Floyd Carlisle and E. Walter Clarke—financed the *Enterprise*. Vanderbilt managed and skippered the *Enterprise*.

Rule changes for 1934 requiring full accommodations for crew and placing wenches above deck adversely affected the yacht. She was broken up for scrap in September 1935 at the Herreshoff boatyard.

SHAMROCK V, THE 1930 CHALLENGER

Designed by Charles Nicholson and built by the Camper & Nicholson yard in Gosport, the *Shamrock V*, was sturdy and well built; her skin was mahogany planking over steel frames, with a yellow pine deck; teak stem, sternposts and counter-timbers; a hollow spruce mast, elliptical section; and a lower sail area but greater rig height relative to other J's. Her waterline length, 81.1 feet, and her overall length, 119.8 feet, with a displacement of 134 tons. *Shamrock V* worked out in extensive tuning in the Solent,[14] racing against the *Shamrock IV* before the 1930 challenge.

Lipton's magnificent J-class flyer the *Shamrock V*
tries out her wings racing in the Solent at Cowes.

CONSTRUCTING THE *SHAMROCK V*

The *Shamrock V* conformed to Lloyd's scantling rules and under the
supervision of the society's surveyors. The keel is elm 10⅜ inches molded
depth. The stern, sternpost, and counter timbers are teak, the planking
mahogany 2.30 inches thick, and the decks of 2.16 inches square white
pine planking, laid to the curve of the boat's side—the covering boards
and king plank being mahogany.

The framework throughout the yacht is steel. The keel plate .48 of an
inch thick, tapering to .33 of an inch at the ends, with vertical keel plate on
each side 12½ inches deep by .28 of an inch thick, forming a longitudinal
trough connected to the keel plate with steel angle bars 2½ inches by 2½
inches by .29 of an inch.

The frames are spaced 18 inches apart, heel to heel, and are 3 inches
by 2½ inches by .27 of an inch, the reverse bars carried up to the cabin

floor level, 2½ inches by 2½ inches by .24 of an inch. The floor plates are 17 inches deep by .25 of an inch.

There are seven pairs of web frames 10 inches deep by .20 of an inch stiffened with face bars 2½ inches by 2½ inches by .22 of an inch.

The sheer strake is 19.70 inches deep by .29 of an inch amidships, tapering to 15.50 inches by .25 of an inch at ends. A bilge strake is fitted outside the frames 12 ½ inches by .28 of an inch with ten diagonal tie plates 6½ inches by .29 of an inch between sheer strake and bilge plate.

The upper and lower deck beams are fitted on alternate frames and on every frame in way of mast. The main deck beams are 4½ inches by 3 inches by .90 of an inch amidships, reduced gradually to 3½ inches by 2½ inches by .20 of an inch at each end of the Bessel. They are connected to the frames with riveted brackets, and intermediate brackets are fitted to each frame, further connecting the sheer strake and main deck stringer plate. This stringer plate, which is 19½ inches wide by .31 of an inch amidships tapering to 15½ inches by .27 of an inch at ends is flanged for connection to the sheer strake, the upper deck tie plates are 6½ inches wide by .29 of an inch thick. The lower deck beams are 3 inches by 2½ inches by .25 of an inch and are fitted with a stringer plate 16 inches by .25 of an inch which is flanged up to connect with the heads of the reverse bars. The lower deck tie plates are 5 inches by .25 of an inch fore and aft.

An intercostal keelson is fitted from amidships to the forward end of the water line with double keelson angles above the floor plates, 3 inches by 2½ Inches by .29 of an inch.

The mast step is incorporated with the intercostal keelson and is squared to the rake of the mast, readily to permit slight movement of the mast forward or aft. The sheer strake in way of the mast is increased in depth to 3 feet 6 inches to take the lower palms of the chain plates, because the yacht is fitted with steel channel plates about 16 inches wide to give added spread to the lower rigging.

The rudder blade is mahogany with a bronze stern, which passes up through a fairing below the counter about 3 feet deep. There is a stuffing box inside, close above which is the steering quadrant, which, in turn, is connected to the steering wheel with wire rope and a Hans Renold roller chain.

THE NEWPORT COURSE

The original course of the New York Yacht Club started from the club anchorage off Weehawken and continued down the Hudson to the Upper Bay through The Narrows and around the South West Spit or out around the Sandy Hook lightship, with an acute angled turn at the Spit, a right angle off the Hook. Strong tides prevailed in The Narrows, and sand banks on every side made navigation a challenge. In time, the start moved down to the Upper Bay, between Staten Island and Bay Ridge, a point from which important races as well as the club regattas were sailed.

Rather than Sandy Hook, the racecourse chosen was Rhode Island Sound and Newport Harbor as homeport.

The starting line of the new course was nine miles southeast, from the Brentons Reef Lightship, immediately outside Newport Harbor, and six miles south of Sakonnet Point. This course is almost on a line from Block Island to Gay Head, and so far distant from these islands and the Rhode Island shore to leave a clear sweep for winds from all quarters. The depth of the course varies from fifteen to twenty-two fathoms; the range of tide is about three and a half feet.

September weather was in doubt, but it was reasonably certain that chances for wind off Block Island are greatly superior to those off New York or Marblehead, while the "September Gale" is proverbial on the Rhode Island coast.

The committee reckoned, there, the weather and breezes was likely to be better, and the crowds would be easier to control. Excitement reigned supreme in the fashionable old resort town; special rail cars were running from Chicago, the bay and harbor overflowed with yachts, the narrow waterfront streets were clogged with traffic, blimps floated in the sky, and bay ferries doubled their schedules transporting curious tourists.

⌒ RULES OF THE MATCH ⌒

Conditions governing the races as agreed upon by the committees of the Royal Ulster Yacht club and the New York Yacht Club follow—slightly abridged for length.

DATES OF RACES. The first race shall be sailed on Saturday, September 13, 1930, and the races shall be sailed on every succeeding weekday, provided, however, that immediately on the conclusion of each race the race committee shall inquire of each contestant whether he is willing to start the next day. Should either contestant reply in the negative, one day shall intervene before starting the next race, Sunday shall not count as such intervening day.

NUMBER OF RACES. The best four out of seven races shall decide the match.

COURSES. Races shall be started from a mark anchored nine nautical miles S.E. (Magnetic) from the Brentons Reef light vessel.

FIRST, THIRD, FIFTH, AND SEVENTH RACES — Fifteen nautical miles to windward or leeward and return.

SECOND, FOURTH, AND SIXTH RACES — A triangle with approximately ten nautical miles to the side.

All races to be started to windward if in the opinion of the race committee it is possible. The compass direction of the courses to be signaled as early as possible, and the tug bearing the marks to be started not less than ten minutes prior to the warning signal.

SIGNALS. The warning signal shall be made ten minutes before the start. Five minutes after the warning signal the preparatory signal shall be made. Five minutes after the preparatory signal the starting signal shall be made. The time of the starting signal shall be taken as the time of the start of both yachts.

START. The warning signal shall be given as nearly as practical at 10:30 A.M. No race shall be started after 12:30 P.M.

POSTPONEMENTS. If in the opinion of the race committee the weather shall be, at the time appointed for the start of any race, or threaten to be, of such severe character as not to afford a reasonable opportunity of fairly testing the speed of the two yachts, the race may be postponed, unless either contestant shall insist upon its being started.

TIME LIMIT. If in any race neither yacht goes over the course in five and a half hours, such race shall not count and shall be resailed.

UNFINISHED RACES. An unfinished race or one resulting in a tie shall be repeated until finished.

NYYC RULES GOVERN. The measurement, scantling and racing rules of the New York Yacht Club, as the same now exist, shall govern the races, except insofar as the same may be inconsistent with this agreement.

FIXTURES AND FITTINGS. Doors, bulkheads, galley, and forecastle fixtures and fittings need not be carried. A water tank or tanks of the aggregate capacity of 400 gallons shall be carried. The usual plumbing appurtenances to the number of three shall be installed and carried.

MAINSAILS. Mainsails shall be jib-headed.

TIME ALLOWANCE. There shall be no time allowance.

RATING. Yachts shall not rate over 76 feet.

The following unemotional descriptions of the first two races are observations by novelist Alec Waugh, who acknowledges being a neither a sailor nor a sport writer.

The first race was won by *Enterprise*. It was a straight there-and-back race. Owing to a shift of wind, there was no windward leg, and in the opinion of that sound judge, Herbert L. Stone, there was no reason why good sailing should not have won the race for *Shamrock*. It was a race that in point of fact told little. Harold Vanderbilt said afterwards that it was a good race and the

Shamrock was a fast yacht. Lipton's comment was, "If I were not disappointed I should be in a mental home. I'd be more optimistic of getting first prize if the last boat over the finish were victor."

Waugh continues with his succinct report of the second race.

It was the second race that was decisive. It was a foggy day, with the yellow lightship off the reef standing out in contrast against a grey-blue background. The racers faded away as dream ships in the mist, and the guests on the *Erin* had to listen to the race by wireless. Probably very few of them realized what was happening out there in the fog. The first leg of the race was the first trial to windward, and the superiority of the *Enterprise* at every point [of sailing] showed that the outcome of the series was not in any doubt. As Stone says, "The crew of the *Enterprise* knew it and the crew of the *Shamrock* must have sensed it."

Sport writers' reports about the 1930-Cup races express almost universal agreement that they were far less exciting than the trials. Edwin P. Hoyt, in his 1969 book, *The Defenders*, quotes one reporter as describing the first race as "the dullest race sailed in American waters [Rhode Island Sound] all year."

Captain Vanderbilt took *Enterprise* out in front at the start and led all the way, finishing 2 minutes and 52 seconds ahead. *Enterprise* won the second race by more than 9 minutes. *Shamrock V* made a better start in the third race, and managed to blanket *Enterprise* for a few minutes, but Vanderbilt tacked away from his opponent, cleared his wind, and began to edge ahead. Then *Shamrock's* main halyard gave away, and the mainsail sagged. The race was over, *Shamrock* having to default. The fourth race was sailed in the best wind of the series at 14 knots over a triangular course. The crew of *Enterprise* noticed a change in the wind before the *Shamrock* and got off to a fine start, increasing the lead until at the halfway mark the defender was 9 minutes and 10 seconds ahead. She loafed home, letting *Shamrock V* catch up a bit, and still won the race by 5 minutes and 44 seconds, to finish the series of 1930.

Sport writer Sidney B. Whipple writes the following in the September 16, 1930 issue of the *Prescott Arizona Journal Miner*:

American Boat Takes *Shamrock* in Second Race: *Enterprise* Has margin of Two Races for American [*sic*] Cup.

Newport, R.I., Sept. 15 (UP) Harold S. Vanderbilt sailed his yacht *Enterprise* to victory by a margin of nine minutes and 34 seconds today over Sir Thomas Lipton's *Shamrock* and with the victory established an impressive margin in favor of the American boat.

Enterprise now has won two races. It needs but two more to send the *Shamrock* back to England in defeat without the historic America's Cup for which it challenged.

The margin of two races to none in favor of the *Enterprise* was only a portion of the advantage Vanderbilt apparently demonstrated today that he was capable of meeting and defeating the challenging yacht and crew at almost any branch of racing.

On the start, he out-jockeyed the green boat from the Royal Ulster Yacht Club and its master, Capt. Edward Heard, getting such a start across the line that in ten minutes he was in position to cross the *Shamrock's* bows at any time he chose.

When he finally did cross the bows and *Shamrock* went to the opposite tack to escape the disadvantage of having the *Enterprise* on the windward, Vanderbilt followed and it didn't take long for him to demonstrate that he did not propose to let *Shamrock* get away for a moment.

When the windward beat of the 30-mile triangular course off Brenton's Reef had been completed, Vanderbilt out sailed Heard and the green yacht again in rounding the marking buoy and from then on the race was as good as over. The American skipper set great billows of sail and scudded before the wind, opening yard after yard of water between himself and the Britisher and on the final run home, despite difficulty in holding a light breeze for a time, the story was that same.

When the American boat sailed over the finish line amid the throaty blasts of a hundred yachts and powerboats, the *Shamrock* could just barely be seen, almost two miles behind.

The third and final race is described in a single paragraph written by novelist Michael D'Antonio.

Thanks to perfect sailing, *Shamrock V* stole the lead in the start of the third race and Sir Thomas's spirits rose, *Enterprise* caught up before they reached the halfway point of the race, and the contest seemed to be very close. Then, suddenly, the main cord securing *Shamrock V's* sail snapped. The canvas started flapping, and some of it fell into the water. Vanderbilt noticed the breakdown and circled back to make sure no one had been injured or knocked overboard. When he was assured that everyone on the challenger was safe, he sailed on to an easy victory. As a black tugboat came to retrieve *Shamrock V*, her owner tried to encourage his friends aboard the *Erin* with a few jokes and brave talk, but at least one of his guests was so disappointed she went below decks to cry.

Harold S. Vanderbilt stands proudly at the wheel of his champion J-class yacht the *Enterprise*.

CHAPTER FIFTEEN

The Finishing Touch

The following three articles are from the October 4, 1930 issue of *The Pathfinder* by an anonymous author.

Shamrock Fails to Win a Race
The American Defender, *Enterprise*, Superior in Every Way
Takes Four Straight Races from Sir Thomas Lipton's Yacht.

In his fifth attempt in 30 years to win the America's Cup, Sir Thomas Lipton not only suffered defeat but also humiliation as his *Shamrock V* trailed Harold Vanderbilt's *Enterprise* in four straight races. Both the American yacht and the American skipper showed superiority in every velocity of wind.

The *Shamrock V* lost the third race after a run of five miles when her main halyard parted and the mainsail collapsed. The first race was the closest, the challenger finishing the 30 mile triangular course just three minutes behind the defender. The best time for the course was three hours, 10 minutes and 13 seconds, made the fourth race. Sir Thomas was hardly disappointed more than thousands of American friends and well-wishers who admired his sportsmanship. He repeated that he was beaten with the utmost fairness, but there was a general feeling among his companions that it is just about hopeless to try to win the Cup with a yacht that must be heavy enough to sail across the Atlantic.

This fifth effort of Sir Thomas was just like three of his others in his failure to win a single race. In 1920, the *Shamrock IV* won two races, one of which was due to an accident to the defender. Looking forlornly at his boat as it trailed the *Enterprise* Sir Thomas exclaimed, "She's not the boat she was when we raced in England; she's nowhere near as fast, but I have no alibi, no excuse. The weather has been just what we wanted; something very unusual seems to have happened to her. She seems dead under her sails." As his hopes went glimmering in the last race, the old skipper seemed to lose courage. "No single man in England," he exclaimed, "can build a million-dollar yacht alone. Hereafter it will have to be syndicate against syndicate."

While Sir Thomas declared everything fair, some of those close to him seemed to feel a little different about it. His secretary, John Westwood, remarked that the *Enterprise* "had all kinds of things which we never heard nor dreamed of." He added, "Now if we challenged again how would we know what you were going to invent? You make it too difficult. It is not like our kind of yachting."

There were many improvements in the *Enterprise*, which was much the more costly boat. Its hollow mast of duralumin weighed some 1,200 pounds less than the wooden mast of the *Shamrock*. To this mast, Sir Thomas attributed his defeat. The [so-called] "Bermuda rigging," used for the first time, allowed the mainsail to reach to the tip of the mast. New rigging, new methods of controlling the sails and many other details were developed to save weight and give greater efficiency. *Enterprise* was six and a half tons lighter than the *Shamrock*.

One big advantage the American yacht had was the skill of its skipper Harold Vanderbilt. He showed himself distinctly superior to skipper Ted Heard of the *Shamrock*.

THE VICTOR —

"A darned fine fellow," is Sir Thomas Lipton's characterization of Harold S. Vanderbilt, skipper of the victorious *Enterprise*, the Yacht that Sir Thomas now calls "the marvel of the seven seas." It is quite appropriate that this sea-going member of the wealthy Vanderbilt family has Sterling for a middle name. Only 48 years old, he is a veteran yachtsman and is loath to quit his own yacht, the *Vara*, even for business. But, he doesn't have to; he is a capitalist and can well afford to pursue this rich man's sport.

Born at Oakdale, N.Y., the son of William Kissam Vanderbilt, he inherited wealth, got his A.B. at Harvard, and attended Harvard Law. As soon as he quit school, a place was made for him with the New York Central Railroad and it is only natural that he should now be a director of that line and its subsidiaries. Like the other Vanderbilts, he has had time and opportunity to go down to the sea in yachts and because of this knowledge was commissioned a lieutenant (junior grade) in the naval reserve at the outbreak of the World War. He saw active service, rising to commanding officer of Scout Patrol No. 56, and later section commander of the submarine chaser detachment stationed at Queenstown. Ireland.

Not only is Harold Vanderbilt an able mariner, but he takes his victory over the *Shamrock V* very quietly. He has yet to offer any criticism of his rival, being content to say, "Boats are deceptive–you can't always be too sure!"

—AND THE VANQUISHED

In being again defeated in his attempt to lift the America's Cup, isn't Sir Thomas Lipton entitled to some sort of a cup for an endurance record? "You had it for 78 years—ever since I was a two-year-old," this veteran challenger wisecracks. "I don't see what use you have for it anyway; you've nothing to put in it any more."

Sir Thomas, who has already spent $10,000,000 building yachts and trying to get the $500 pewter [The writer errs: the Cup is British sterling.] Cup back home, is such a jolly good sport that probably a majority of Americans, either secretly or openly wished him success this year. America is also sympathetic to Sir Thomas because, being a tradesman, he was blackballed for membership in the British Royal Yacht Club.

"The Americans have always beaten me fairly and squarely," Lipton proclaimed. That sort of sportsmanship endears him the more to Americans, especially since the former unsuccessful British contenders for the Cup kept on constant bickering, went home, and accused the American skippers of everything but murder.

That Sir Thomas has a sense of humor, as well as an eye in advertising, was shown when, in talking to the mayor of Boston, he said, "I have always believed that Boston had the most intelligent people; they threw the tea overboard when they found it wasn't Lipton's." Thus does his frankly and good naturally deal with the allegation that he has made his quest of the America's Cup a paying proposition in spite of constant defeats. That the publicity he got for his tea was worth far more than he has paid for yachts. There is no better way for Sir Thomas to handle that subject than to openly jest about it.

In fact, Sir Thomas is a merchant prince with a fabulous fortune. After acquiring some 600 stores in England and Scotland, he bought up great plantations in Ceylon and elsewhere and began to grow his own tea and coffee. He even has a packinghouse in Omaha, Nebraska.

"Business is my vocation, yachting is my hobby," Remarked Sir Thomas, and he added that though his hobby had yielded him many happy hours it had also yielded him "a few disappointments."

However, through it all Sir Thomas continues to insist that, "honest tea is the best policy."

1930 AND BEYOND

D URING THE SUMMER OF 1931, visions of one last attempt at challenging for the Cup burned in Lipton's imagination. He entered into talks with the New York Yacht Club for the sixth time, and the Club board thought it reasonable this time to offer a series of concessions to lessen the burden of the cost of building new racers. Remember, at this time the world was in the throws of the great economic depression. While the wealthy members of the New York Yacht Club could well afford the titanic expense of designing and building a new defender, rational thinkers agreed that an ostentatious display of wealth would appear offensive to a suffering public.

The new plan allowed both *Shamrock V* and the *Enterprise* to meet again with a few strategic alterations. The *Enterprise* must abandon her aluminum mast, relocate below-deck winches to topside, and build crew accommodations. The renegotiated rules allowed Lipton to modify the *Shamrock V* bringing her up to top-notch performance.

On October 2, 1931, after a four-day bout with a respiratory infection that his 81-year-old body could not fight off, Sir Tom died peacefully in his sleep at his home.

Lipton's estate sold the *Shamrock V* to Thomas O. M. Sopwith in 1932. Sopwith modified the yacht's hull and rudder; he later sold her to Sir Richard Fairey, who after the war sold her to Mario Crespi. Crespi who in turn sold her to Piero Scanu in 1962, and Scanu renamed her *Quattrofoglio* (spelling uncertain but roughly "Four Leaf" in Italian as a play on her original name). By this time, she may have become ketch rigged. She was again rebuilt at Camper & Nicholson in 1967–70 and sold to the Lipton Tea Company in 1986. The tea company later donated her to the Newport (Rhode Island) Museum of Yachting. In 1989, Elizabeth Meyer restored the rig, bulwarks and deckhouse to original specifications and in 1995 sold her to the Newport Yacht Restoration School, which in 1998, sold her to the Newport *Shamrock V* Corporation. She underwent another refitting in 2000 at Pendennis, under Gerard Dykstra, who sold her to Marcos de Maraes of Brazil. Maraes sails her today as a pleasure yacht.

APPENDIX

Chronological Highlights of the Herreshoff Manufacturing Company

JBH = John Brown Herreshoff, NGH = Nathanael Greene Herreshoff

1863　JBH at age 22, set up a shop in Bristol, Rhode Island to build boats for a living, helped by various family members, and briefly by a partner, Dexter Stone.

1864　NGH, at 16, models his first wood boats, the *Henrietta*, the *Haidee*, the *Violet*, and the *Ariel*. The boy's father Charles, a meticulous tinkerer, developed a sliding ballast box and continued to train his sons in the proper care of a boat.

1866　NGH enters M.I.T., studies mechanical engineering.

1868　NGH designs his first steamer.

1869　NGH begins work as a designer for the Corliss Steam Engine Company in Providence, RI.

1870　NGH designs his first catamaran, the *Amaryllis*, in the summer, he sails her to New York and defeats all comers.

1876　NGH designs his first famous racing sailboat, the *Shadow*, which is built by JBH.

1876　NGH designs the first US Navy torpedo boat, the 57-foot, *Lightning*.

1877　NGH designs his first major vessel the 120-foot *Estelle* including all the vessel's propelling machinery for gun-running Cuban rebels

1878　JBH and NGH form the Herreshoff Manufacturing Co., their early specialty is steam yachts.

1891　NGH designs and JBH builds the racing sloop *Gloriana*; at the end of her first season of sailing the yachting fraternity hails her as a "break-through" yacht.

1891   NGH designs the first fin-keel sailboat, the *Dilemma*, and has her built for his personal use.

1893   The first three metal-hulled sailing yachts, the *Navahoe*, *Colonia*, and *Vigilant*, all about 85 feet LWL, are designed and built by HMCo; the last two become America's Cup contenders.

1893   NGH steers the *Vigilant* to victory in the America's Cup race against the *Valkyrie II*.

1895   The *Defender* designed by NGH and built at HMC defends and wins the America's Cup.

1895   NGH designs and HMC builds the largest (175' 6" LOA) all steel, ocean-going power vessels, the USN torpedo boats the *DuPont* and the *Porter*.

1903   NGH designs and HMC builds the largest Cup Defender ever built; the *Reliance,* she is overwhelmingly successful against Lipton's *Shamrock III*.

1904   NGH writes a new rating rule for racing yachts encouraging more practical hull shapes & sizes.

1915   JBH dies shortly after a disagreement with NGH about a contract to build torpedo boats for the Russian government. Ownership of HMC passes to New York investors when JBH's heirs sell their stock in the company; soon after NGH sells his stock in the company.

1924   Rudolf F. Haffenreffer buys principal assets of the HMC at auction and continues boat building.

1924   NGH in semi-retirement is retained as consultant, his son Sidney is chief designer and engineer.

1938   NGH Dies on June 2, 1938, at age 90.

1944   The HMC under control of Rudolf F. Haffenreffer and family build 100 USN fighting ships.

1945   Haffenreffer closes the HMC, sells machinery, donates drawings and records to M.I.T., and tears down the waterfront construction sheds. The Herreshoff Marine Museum and NGH's grandson Halsey C. Herreshoff now own most of the property.

Nathanael Greene Herreshoff is one of the world's most revered designers of sail and steam powered watercraft. In his more than 2,000 designs, Captain Nat introduced scores of innovative devices to yachting. Added to his successful six Cup-winning designs, additionally, the Bristol, Rhode Island based Herreshoff Manufacturing Company built the 1930 and 1934 Cup defenders.

Karen C. Delgado's 1996 characterization of the author.

About the Author

RICHARD V. SIMPSON IS a native Rhode Islander who has always lived within walking distance to Narragansett Bay, first in the Edgewood section of Cranston and then in Bristol, where he has lived since 1960.

A graphic designer by trade, he worked in advertising, printing, display, and textile design studios. He designed and built parade floats for Kaiser Aluminum's Bristol plant and the U.S. Navy in Newport, Rhode Island. After retiring in 1996 from a twenty-nine-year federal civil service career with the U.S. Navy Supply Center and Naval Undersea Warfare Center, he began a second career as an author of books on subjects of historical interest in Rhode Island's East Bay with his principal focus on Bristol.

Richard and his wife Irene are antique dealers doing business as *Bristol Art Exchange*; they received their Rhode Island retail sales license in 1970.

Beginning in 1985, Richard acted as a contributing editor for the national monthly *Antiques & Collecting Magazine* in which eighty-five of his articles have appeared.

Bristol's famous Independence Day celebration and parade was Richard's first venture in writing a major history narrative. His 1989 *Independence Day: How the Day is Celebrated in Bristol, Rhode Island* is the singular authoritative book on the subject; his many anecdotal Fourth of July articles have appeared in the local *Bristol Phoenix* and the *Providence Journal*. His history of Bristol's Independence Day celebration is the source of a story in the July 1989 *Yankee Magazine* and July 4, 2010 issue of *Parade Magazine*.

BOOKS BY RICHARD V. SIMPSON

A History of the Italian-Roman Catholic Church in Bristol, RI (1967)

Independence Day: How the Day is Celebrated in Bristol, RI (1989)

Old St. Mary's: Mother Church in Bristol, RI (1994)

Bristol, Rhode Island: In the Mount Hope Lands of King Philip (1996)

Portsmouth, Rhode Island, Pocasset: Ancestral Lands of the Narragansett (1997)

Tiverton and Little Compton, Rhode Island: Pocasset and Sakonnet (1997)

Tiverton and Little Compton, Rhode Island: Volume II (1998)

Bristol, Rhode Island: The Bristol Renaissance (1998)

America's Cup Yachts: The Rhode Island Connection (1999)

Building the Mosquito Fleet: U.S. Navy's First Torpedo Boats (2001)

Bristol: Montaup to Poppasquash (2002)

Bristol, Rhode Island: A Postcard History (2005)

Narragansett Bay: A Postcard History (2005)

Herreshoff Yachts: Seven Generations (2007)

Historic Bristol: Tales from an Old Rhode Island Seaport (2008)

The America's Cup: Trials and Triumphs (2010)

The Quest for the America's Cup: Sailing to Victory (2012)

Tiverton & Little Compton Rhode Island: Historic Tales of the Outer Plantations (2012)

Historic Tales of Colonial Rhode Island: Aquidneck Island and the Founding of the Ocean State (2012)

Preserving Bristol: Restoring, Reviving, and Remembering (2014)

Bibliography

Capen, Oliver Bronson; *Country Life in America*, Vol. IV, No. 4, August 1903.

DiAntonio, Michael; *A Full Cup*, Riverside Books, New York, 2010.

Hammond, Geoffrey F.; *Showdown at Newport*, Walden Publications, 1974.

Herreshoff, L. Francis; *An Introduction to Yachting*, Sheridan House, New York, 1963.

Herreshoff, Nathanael G.; *Recollections*, Edited by Carlton J. Pinheiro, Herreshoff Marine Museum, 1998.

Hoyt, Edwin P.; *The Defenders*, A. S. Barnes and Company, New York, 1969.

Kenealy, A.J.; *Leslie's Weekly* [Magazine], September 21, 1901.

Scientific American, July 8; August 12; September 16; September 23; October 7; October 14; October 21, 1899

Scientific American March 30; April 13; May 11; May 18; June 22; June 28; July 11, 1901

Scientific American April 11; April 25; May 9; May 30; June 20; June 27; August 29, 1903

Stephens, W. P.; *The Match for the America's Cup—1930*, Supplement to *The Sportsman*, Vol. VII, No. V, Boston.

Swan, William U.; *The America's Cup*, *The Sketch Book Magazine*, Vol. 7, No. 11, September 1930.

Waugh, Alec; *The Lipton Story*, Doubleday & Company, 1950.

Endnotes

1. Everyone who is a fan of the America's Cup races is forever grateful that Stevens did not name the schooner for his hometown, Hoboken! Heaven forbid, the Hoboken Cup!

2. Bristol Phoenix – September 1898: The *Defender* is being brought home [from Glen Island] and will be completely overhauled and put in first class shape [as a trial horse] for the [1899 defender] trial races. The *Defender's* topsides will be removed and it is understood that a thicker plating of aluminum will replace the plating now on, the present aluminum plating being more or less corroded.

   New deck beams of aluminum will also be substituted for the beams now in this yacht, which are of aluminum and which are corroded.

3. Lord Dunraven had come closer than any previous Englishman had to winning back the Cup. Many will agree that *Valkyrie II* was the faster boat. The NYYC entry saved the Cup, but by the most narrow margin and only by the most dauntless seamanship, against what may have been a superior vessel. The next year, the *Vigilant* went to English waters to race against *Valkyrie II's* sister ship, the Prince of Wales's *Britannia*. In seventeen meetings, the *Britannia* won twelve to *Vigilant's* five wins.

4. *Bristol Phoenix*—July 28, 1894: It matters not whether the *Vigilant* be a winner or loser in the number of races over the other side of the water, it will not detract from the splendid victories heretofore won by the Herreshoffs in the numerous races in which the English sportsmen have sent their crack yachts and been defeated.

   It must be remembered that although the Herreshoffs are the builders of the *Vigilant*, she is owned by a gentleman who never was a true sportsman. It is [Jay] Gould, the owner, who is the loser or winner. Let the Prince of Wales bring the *Britannia* to Newport next season and if there is not more than an even score in the settlement won by the Yankees in their own waters, then they will settle down to the fact that "Britannia rules the waves," but not until then. There is no doubt that the *Vigilant* has been handicapped in every way and it is doubtful if she is in as fine a racing trim as she was last season. Then taking into consideration the perfect understanding they have of the tides that prevail in those waters, it must be conceded that there is a chance of her being beaten by an English skipper whose experience is unquestioned.

5. In later years, the Ratsey family was the renounced makers of the famous English sails.

6. Captain Charlie Barr is remembered as an aggressive skipper for his ability for finding the most favorable position, during the pre-start run up to the starting line, putting his opponent at a great disadvantage.

7. Used with permission of the Herreshoff Museum & America's Cup Hall of Fame, Bristol, Rhode Island, www.herreshorff.org.

8. For a discussion of some technical aspects of advancements in racing yacht's designs, the reader is directed to *America's Cup: Trials & Triumphs*, The History Press, 2010.

9. In the *Defender* Herreshoff developed the fin keel idea. Her construction was of both aluminum and bronze, 2 feet shorter, over all, than the *Vigilant*, but 2.3 feet longer on the water line; she had about 3 feet less beam and 6 feet more draft. From the beginning of trials with the *Vigilant*, she showed superiority on every point of sailing, and chosen to meet the newcomer, *Valkyrie III*.

George Lennox Watson had designed the boat, like her predecessors in the last two matches. She was a much larger and more powerful vessel than her namesake of 1898, and her sail area was even greater than that of the *Defender*.

The antagonists had very nearly reached the common type to which they were approaching for almost a decade. When the boats were measured it was found that for the first time in the struggles between "single-stickers" time allowance had to be given by the challenger to the defender, At 30-knot races had been decided, the *Valkyrie* allowed 28 seconds handicap.

10. According to Edwin P. Hoyt in his 1969 book, *The Defenders*, because of the troublesome spectator vessels that vexed Lord Dunraven, a fleet of US Coast Guard revenue cutters and US Navy torpedo boats were deployed to keep unauthorized craft away from the racecourse.

11. Under these rules, Captain Barr decided to make a late start for in running off the wind this would give his yacht a chance to blanket his competitor and sometimes pass her, thus making the best time over the course.

12. As a designer of yachts, Bowdoin Bradlee Crowninshield is remembered for his long, sleek 'knockabout' sloops, 2 Americas Cup contenders and a number of successful racing schooners built at his shipyard in Somerset, Massachusetts.

13. The Park Avenue boom was fitted with novel color-coded pegs and holes to guide the crew as they attached the sail in different configurations.

14. The Solent is a channel of water separating the Isle of Wight from Hampshire on the English mainland. It is approximately fourteen miles long with an average width of three miles. It narrows at the eastern end and to a greater extent at the western end.